W9-CFZ-110

International Federation of Library Associations and Institutions
Fédération Internationale des Associations de Bibliothécaires et des Bibliothèques
Internationaler Verband der bibliothekarischen Vereine und Institutionen
Международная Федерация Библиотечных Ассоциаций и Учреждений
Federación Internacional de Asociaciones de Bibliotecarios y Bibliotecas

IFLA Publications 104

Cost Management
for University Libraries

with attached CD-ROM

Klaus Ceynowa and André Coners

in collaboration with
Roswitha Poll, Peter te Boekhorst, Britta Pouwels
and Burkard Rosenberger

Translated from the German
by Patrick Nicholson

K · G · Saur   München 2003

IFLA Publications
edited by Sjoerd Koopman

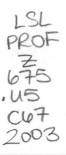

Recommended catalogue entry:

Cost Management for University Libraries
[International Federation of Library Associations and Institutions].
Klaus Ceynowa and André Coners, in collaboration with Roswitha Poll,
Peter te Boekhorst, Britta Pouwels and Burkard Rosenberger
– München : Saur, 2003, 177 p. 21 cm
   (IFLA publications ; 104)
   ISBN 3-598-21834-6

Bibliographic information published by Die Deutsche Bibliothek
Die Deutsche Bibliothek lists this publication in the Deutsche Nationalbibliografie;
detailed bibliographic data is available in the Internet at
http://dnb.ddb.de.

Printed on acid-free paper
The paper used in this publication meets the minimum requirements of American National
Standard for Information Sciences – Permanence of Paper for Printed Library Materials,
ANSI Z39.48.1984.

Printed / Bound by Strauss Offsetdruck, Mörlenbach

ISBN 3-598-21834-6
ISSN 0344-6891 (IFLA Publications)

Table of Contents

Foreword

This handbook documents the results of the project, „Cost Management for University Libraries", that was sponsored by the „Deutsche Forschungsgemeinschaft". The project was carried out by the University and Regional Library of Münster in cooperation with the University and Regional Library of Düsseldorf and the University Library of Paderborn. The goal of the project was the development of a cost- and results accounting adapted to the general fiscal framework for key service institutions at universities. This should enable university libraries to achieve more transparent cost of services and to obtain least-cost use of their resources.

Hereby, the issue dealt with does not only apply to libraries in the upcoming years, but also all university institutions. Financial autonomy, global budget, budgeting, decentralized accountability of resources - those and other keywords of the present reform discussion characterize the transition from an appropriation of funds coordinated by budgetary items and position charts to a budgeting oriented on the cost of services rendered. An essential step on the way to output oriented management is the introduction of a university cost accounting, in German universities.

The objective of this handbook is to support university libraries in realizing the described development. In the long-term, libraries will only be successful in the struggle for allocation of funds if they can prove cost efficiency of their work and if their demand for funds is supported by an economically founded product calculation. This cannot be done by the means of traditional cameralism, it rather requires the construction of a library cost accounting. Furthermore, a cost accounting can increase the possibilities of in-house cost management considerably if it is designed in a decision oriented way. For that purpose, information is necessary to disclose the cost-driving factors of service processes and thus, to allow a controlling access. The consistent economical use of available resources is an unalterable condition if libraries want to master new challenges, particularly in the area of digital information services.

The accounting model developed in the project offers an orientational framework to introduce university libraries as well as public institutions in general to this relevant - but still uncommon - topic. The concept presented is not designed as a ridged instruction to be merely followed by the user. It should rather be seen as an open system that can be flexibly adapted to given calculation and management goals. By this means, the transferability - explicitly wished for in the project assignment - of the project results to other central and local operational centers of the university is facilitated.

Without the appropriate software support, the construction of a cost accounting cannot be done efficiently. The use of a spreadsheet does not seem very promising, for the necessary steps of programming and calculation algorithms quickly lead to an obscure complicated program structure that no longer can be understood by a third party. The suggested alternative is the use of standard business administrational software for controlling and cost accounting. However, this type of product is presently only installed at a few universities, a situation that - looking at the price and the trouble of implementation - is not going to change in the near future. Thus, the software tool LIBRARY-MANAGER, which illustrates all steps of the construction of the library cost accounting, was developed in the project. LIBRARYMANAGER is a Windows-based software fulfilling modern standards. Simple serviceability and a comfortable report function were particularly emphasized during its programming. LIBRARYMANAGER essentially accelerates and facilitates the construction and use of the cost accounting. The software is found on the CD-ROM enclosed in this volume.

The University and Regional Library of Münster undertook this project as a logical continuation of its research on performance measurement. In cooperation with mainly international partners and projects, the path went from determining the missions and goals, to evaluating the services with standardized performance indicators, user and staff surveys. These methods helped to evaluate the quality of services, but not the cost-effectiveness. A high standard of service can be connected with high costs; the goal, however, should be effectiveness combined with economical use or resource.

Our thanks goes in the first place to the DFG, whose sponsorship enabled the project. Thanks is also given to the partner universities in Düsseldorf and Paderborn, and, above all to the project managers Ute Olliges-Wieczorek and Martin Karlowitsch in Düsseldorf and Anne May and Susanne Bielefeld in Paderborn. Harald Buch, Sebastian Mundt, and Julia Unsöld gave manifold support during the project and the edition of this volume. A special thanks goes to Gerrit von der Hardt and Tobias Wuth for their contribution to the creation of LIBRARYMANAGER. Dr. Reinhold Mayer, Horváth & Partner GmbH, gave essential support to the project through critical and stimulating discussion about methodical principles. Last but not least, our hearty thanks goes to the staff of the libraries involved in the project. Without them, a project like this could not be successful.

1 Basic Principles of Cost Accounting for University Libraries

1.1 Why Cost Analysis of Library Services?

University libraries ensure the supply of information for research, teaching, and studies. The financial framework in which they are working is presently in a transformation process. On the one hand, the constantly tense financial situation of the universities limits their scope of action, on the other hand, users' demands are growing as regards the extent and quality of services. The main task of library management in the coming years can therefore be reduced to the simple formula: To master an increasingly differentiated and widening spectrum of services with always less resources.

Higher demand is in the first place due to the still unrestricted growth of scientific information, both in the form of printed and digital publications. In connection with qualified electronic instruments for search, reference, and document supply, this means that there is a clear and continual increasing intensification of use. The unchanged high and tendentiously further growing number of students accelerates this development.

In addition to that, there is also the paradigm change of library services described by the term *virtual library*. The acquisition and provision of conventional media, especially printed publications, is augmented and tendentiously overlain by the use of digitalized information. This information is intangible and site independent, and can be manipulated. For libraries this means new tasks with new and intensive demands for staff and equipment. When libraries offer a „virtual library" there will be a fundamental shift in their processes. In addition to the collection of physical information carriers „on site", libraries have to offer comfortable access to remote digital documents and data resources. This development has led to a clear increase of technology costs for equipment, infrastructure of the network, and long distance data transfer. Expense cutting in the library's acquisition budget is, on the other hand, only to be expected if library consortia can obtain more favorable license contracts, or if paying per access takes the place of buying and subscribing.

Facing these increasing tasks is a university library funding that is, to a large extent, felt as inadequate. Because of the roll-over of budgets practiced in many places for years, the acquisition funds are stagnating or are even on the decline. The price inflation, especially in the area of journals, can often only be absorbed by rigid cancellations (Griebel/Tscharntke 1998, 30ff.). Moreover, replacement freezes for staff and staff cuts let it appear questionable whether libraries have sufficient staff capacities to compete with private suppliers on the growing market of electronic information services.

The critical financial situation of the university budgets focuses the interest on economic management instruments that promise to combine cost cutting potential and the optimal allocation of resources. With their help, the universities should succeed in orienting their actions more than ever on the criteria of economic and cost efficiency. The sponsors' and the decision makers' interest is not only directed at the provision of services in faculties and institutes, but also especially at central units like university libraries, computer centers, and university administration. These make up the universities' so-called indirect service areas. They fulfill support functions for faculties and institutes, which for their part directly deal with the rendering of services in research and teaching. Central units support the creation of value, but do not themselves directly add value. The „service processes" (Küpper 1997, 578) they offer are under particular legitimating pressure, when resources are scarce: Funding institutions want to know what results may be expected for given funds; and they want to be able to make comparisons to see whether the same service can be rendered with lower costs, maybe by commercial suppliers.

But how can it be determined, whether and to what degree libraries are working economically? The principle of economic efficiency, as defined in the national budget regulations, refers to a means-end relation: The aim is the most favorable relation between resources used and results achieved. The best means-end relation involves either achieving a predetermined result using as little funds as possible (minimality principle), or achieving the best possible result with a predetermined budget (maximality principle). Thus, economic efficiency measures the relation of a produced service to the necessary use of resources, and refers to the efficiency of the service production. In academic libraries, whose fundamental tasks are clearly defined, economic efficiency is above all seen in the aspect of the minimality principle.

For managing and controlling the allocation of resources, most university libraries presently are dependent on the cameralistic system, which represents a mere statement of resource and expenditure. The juxtaposition of the budget estimate and the expenditure actually done serves to control the budget implementation and the correctness of cash payment orders and cash transactions. The primary purpose of the cameralistic account is to furnish proof that the funds allocated to an administrative unit - defined by the budget heading - were spent in accordance with the purpose. Thus it checks the legitimacy of resource allocation, not its effectiveness. Accounting procedures in the budget heading merely show the amount of funds spent, e.g. for the acquisition of literature or equipment, but they cannot show which results were produced by the use of those funds, nor to what extent the production of those results was done efficiently. The cameralistic represents the prototype of the input oriented management of administrative acts: The coordination of financial affairs happens with more or less differentiated budget structure and position charts, while the question: „Which results (the „output") are to be achieved with the available resources?" is neglected (cf. Budäus 1997).

The relationship between the use of resources and the performance results can only be demonstrated by the management instrument of cost accounting and results account, whereby controlling access is also made available. Indeed in the framework of university budgets „costs" are often mentioned, but this term is only seldom used in an economic sense. Looked at in an economic way, cameralistic works exclusively with the factors „disbursement" and „expenditure". A disbursement spot is understood to be every decrease of cash assets that is represented as a reduction of cash on hand or of demand balances at credit institutions. The term „expenditure" has a broader meaning. It refers not only to the outflow of cash or book money, but includes creditary business transactions, the increase of accounts payable and the decrease of accounts receivable. In contrast to the terms „disbursement" and „expenditure", which exclusively serve as a description of financial transactions, the term „costs" describes the resources used and used up in the production process (staff, machines, material, energy, etc.). Costs represent the performance related resource consumption of an accounting period appraised in units of money (cf. Hummel/Männel 1990, 73; Kilger 1992, 23). Cost accounting ascertains the resources consumed in the value added process, values their costs, and assigns them to the products (goods and services). The juxtaposition of costs and services is done in three accounting steps according to the classical construction of cost accounting:

- Cost type accounting collects all costs of the business unit (Which costs arise?)

- Cost center accounting assigns them to the production areas (Where do the costs arise?)

- Cost unit accounting establishes the costs of the products/services (What did the costs arise for?).

Organizational units of a university that introduce a cost accounting gain insight into the cost structures of their services offered. Thus, for example, a library doing cost accounting can answer questions about the cost of one loan, one reference question, answered, one document cataloged,etc. In turn, that kind of data create the basis for economic analysis, e.g. in form of comparisons with other university libraries or with commercial suppliers of information services.

The goal is to gain an overview of the relationship between costs and performance of university services and their causality. Cost accounting is presently being implemented in most states of the German Republic. The projects show the common feature of restricting cost accounting to the explanatory function, in other words to the provision of cost information with the goal of increased cost transparency. In opposition to this, the management function of cost accounting, in other words the deliberate use of generated data to influence level of cost, cost structure, and cost trend of the business unit is little noticed.. For the time being there is no systematic testing of instruments for active cost management. This is usually explained by the generally low state of cost accounting in the university sector. This disregard of the decision supporting functions of cost accounting shows above all in the waiving of the cost unit accounting, in other words in the waiving of the accounting step in which cost accounting, by the evaluation of produced goods, actually becomes results accounting.

Cost unit accounting is primarily seen in the ascertainment of the prime costs of products for the purpose of price calculation. Since universities are not striving towards commercial goals, cost unit accounting is given a low priority: „Marketing decisions and thereby the necessity of the ascertainment of prime cost prices as the primary concern of cost unit accounting is not applicable... for universities" (Kuhnert/Leszczensky 1997, 25). Moreover, the intangible character of the product produced at universities is pointed out. Research and teaching, as well as the central service processes supporting them, are, as it is argued, not physical objects like automobiles and refrigerators, which allow a cost accounting access: „The fact that ... the performance emerging from the production process does not represent material goods and thereby is not easily ascertainable, argues in principle against cost unit accounting forming an integral component of cost accounting at universities. ... Therefore there are no definite objectively recognizable cost units"(Kuhnert/ Leszczensky 1997, 25). This objection, if true, should awaken fundamental doubt about the significance and use of a cost analysis of service „products". The intangibility is namely, as is show in detail in chapter 1.3, an essential characteristic of service in general: In the service process there is no transfer object, that - in the sense of an object that is separable from the production of services - is passed on from the provider to the demander. Services change conditions, but they do not transfer objects. Economics also refers to them, therefore, as „substance less goods" (cf. Hilke 1989, 13).

For a library, this waiving of the costing of produced services means that in the present concepts of university cost accounting it is regarded as one cost area internally not further differentiated. As a rule, only the total costs of the library subdivided by the cost types are shown, but not information about the cost structure of its service areas (user services, collection building, document delivery, etc.). Since libraries provide services for research, teaching, and studies, they are, in regards to cost accounting, seen as indirect cost centers, the costs of which are to be allocated to institutes and faculties directly active in research and teaching - the universities' final cost centers. The present models work with non-uniform and somewhat rough clearing ratios. For instance, in one accounting model the total costs of the library are distributed to the faculties proportionally to the number of staff members active in teaching (Paff 1998, 151). Another model allocates the library costs to teaching units proportional to the faculties' portion of the yearly acquisition expenditures (Kuhnert/Leszczensky 1997, 130). At least the last appears questionable, for not the value, but the number of acquired media binds the capacities of the business processes and thereby represents the factor that drives up costs. If the library is represented as a cost area that is not further broken down internally, cost-performance relations can only be shown in the form of a relatively global ratio. The library's total costs can merely be put in relation to the total number of students or of registered users, to the total amount of loans, or to the annual number of hours open. If those kind of indicators flow into a benchmarking, results will not show informative content. If for example a library is clearly „more expensive" per student than another institution, that does not necessarily refer to a hidden inefficiency of the production of services. It can just as well represent the deliberate decision of the university management for a qualified literature provision above the average. If ratios are used like „library costs per student, per hour open, per loan, etc.", the danger exists that these values are wrongly interpreted as marginal costs. It is then assumed that the library's cost per student would be the costs that would additionally accumulate for each additional student, respectively that would sink in the same proportion with the decline of the enrollment numbers. The library budget would then be adjusted accordingly. It is overlooked that library costs are, for the most part, fixed costs that are due to the building and maintenance of the library's service potential, largely independent of whether a thousand more or a thousand less students are being serviced.

The model developed in the following for cost analysis of a university's information provision therefore deliberately chooses a broader approach. Using the example of university libraries, a *decision oriented accounting model* is developed, the primary purpose of which is not the generation of highly aggregated cost information for external funders and decision makers, but rather the optimizing of the cost situation in the interest of an improved efficiency. It can be assumed that the findings obtained on the basis of university libraries are, with appropriate adaptations, transferable to further central operational and administrational centers of universities (cf. Ceynowa 1997).

If the goal of cost accounting is primarily seen in reaching an optimal resource allocation through planning, management, and control of the costs of library services, it cannot be limited to the assignment of costs to the functional areas and to the produced service units. It is necessary to analyze the emergence of costs, that means tracing them back to those factors that determine the consumption of resources by kind and amount, and thereby cause the costs. By identifying those „cost drivers", it is possible to comprehend in detail the development of library costs during the process of service production. It becomes perceivable how the costs develop along the chain of value added - from the ordering of a document up to the delivery, from media processing up to loan, from loan up to reshelving, from the inquiry up to the question answered. Only the analysis of cost driving factors allows to identify potential for rationalization and cost reduction. If benchmarking shows, for example, that the costs of user services of one library are significantly higher than in comparable libraries, this result can only lead to restructuring measures if, at the same, cost accounting shows what causes the cost difference: Does the unclear catalog situation increase the need for advice and thereby raise staff costs? Or is it interlibrary lending that binds over-proportionally high capacities due to inadequate organization? Or are the procedures of document delivery responsible, if they are carried out by professional staff instead of by assistants?

A cost accounting that not only evaluates the performance results by costs, but that also shows how and through what those costs occur, clearly requires a higher degree of differentiation than an accounting model that is geared to external information needs. Particularly, a detailed cost center structure of all functional areas of the library, as well as an analysis of the service processes running within each cost center, are necessary. For service institutions in general, it is valid that the operating procedures - in other words, activities like

„processing an order", „claiming orders", „producing training material" etc. - represent the actual cost driving factors: Performance requires processes, processes use resources, the use of resources causes costs (cf. Remer 1997, 55f.). The analysis of this relationship shows, moreover, that in regards to service institutions the separation between the created product and the creating process is artificial. As a rule, it is valid for services that the produced service process is identical with the product given to the client (cf. Beinhauer/Schellhaas 1997, 416). For example, the inspection of an automobile simultaneously constitutes a process and a product. Also, the majority of the service-„products" that libraries offer are, as the following sections show, nothing more than the relationship of a series of operating procedures (acquiring a document, processing an order, performing a database search, advising a user etc.). The accounting model must therefore be built in the form of a flexible database, where the basis are the costs of the library's service processes, supplemented by non-procedural calculation objects if necessary. This data-pool does indeed also allow generation of strongly condensed cost values up to the level of the above mentioned ratios, but is primarily constructed for the collection of differentiated cost information for answering questions like:

- How does the cost situation of the service area „media acquisition" change with the establishment of electronic business transactions?

- How does the relationship of used-capacity costs to idle-capacity costs develop in the lending department with the introduction of a self-issuing system?

- To what extent can the staff costs of a departmental library be decreased through the intensified use of part-time help and floating staffers?

- Which costs are additionally caused by the installation of an „electronic" reading-room and should accordingly be taken into consideration in the costing?

- Which capacities are set free for other purposes and which costs totally fall away when a certain service area is outsourced? Are the attainable potentials for cost reduction higher then the prices to be paid when outsourcing?

- Which costs originate in the library by services that are not belonging to the core business of providing information for the university, e.g. legal deposit tasks or exhibitions of rare book collections?

- What is the relation of staff costs to media costs? Or the relation of the costs of media acquisition to those of the user services? How high is the proportion of the library's management and administration costs ("overhead") measured against its total costs?

- How does the reduction or the increase of the number of acquired media effect the capacity requirement and thereby the cost level of the cataloging department?

- Which cost types are to be influenced in the short-run, which in the medium-run or long-run?

Given the fact that processes represent the primary cost drivers in service institutions, the problem of calculating the intangible cost units can also be handled. The fact that universities do not produce any physical objects that costs could be calculated with, does not mean that they can dispense with cost unit accounting and thereby the cost analysis of the produced services. It merely means that cost unit accounting for universities and for service institutions in general has to be done as a process cost accounting. The instrument of process cost accounting, originally developed in the USA under the name Activity Based Costing, is rated in the present economic discussion as the prevailing approach to the ascertainment and management of service costs (cf. Serfling/Jeiter 1995, 322). In the following sections the characteristics of service processes, as well as the instrument of process cost accounting used for their costing, are introduced.

1.2 Goals and Tasks of Cost Accounting

Cost accounting aims at collecting, allocating and documenting incurred or planned costs. This is done by categorizing the occurring costs according to the kind of resource consumed (cost type accounting), and ascertaining the costs of the produced services (cost unit accounting). Thus cost accounting constitutes the basic information for cost management, which means actively organizing and influencing costs. For a decision oriented cost accounting, providing information for cost management represents the primary purpose. Especially the degree of differentiation and the exactness of data collection must be adjusted to this goal. The core task of cost accounting - the support of cost oriented planning, management and control of the operational processes - can be divided up into the following individual goals:

- Cost transparency should significant increase cost awareness and provide information for the consequent economical handling of available resources.

- The calculation of „library products" should allow the entrance into procedures of output oriented budgeting of the library budget, which in the progressive globalization of university budgets will take the place of the traditional input oriented steering by budget headings and position charts.

- Cost and performance comparisons between institutions with the goal of learning from the „best-practice-library" should support cost optimization.

- The analysis of additional costs caused by the introduction of new services (so-called relevant costs) should lay a cost related foundation for dispositions concerning the future library profile, especially in building a „digital library."

- Fees for costed user services, above all in the area of electronic document delivery, should be calculated on a justifiable and comprehensible basis.

- Decisions about own production or outsourcing of library services should be evaluated by cost aspects.

- The evaluation of the work processes in libraries in terms of capacity and costs should disclose points of intervention for a cost oriented optimization of the process structure, e.g. by avoiding change of media, elimination of errors, etc.

- Capacity oriented cost analysis should make the identification of overcapacity and idle-capacity costs possible and make rationalization potentials accessible, above all by the consequent adaptation of the available service potential to the actual service demand.

These goals show, that the production of *cost transparency* represents an essential result, which by itself already justifies the implementation of cost accounting. As long as cameralistic represents the sole accounting instrument, fiscal considerations inevitably limit themselves to those budget headings that administrate the available current funds. The staff costs contained in the position chart are only known in a broad outline; still less is known about operating costs and the costs of the premises and investments that are often centrally administrated. With the development of a cost accounting, university libraries obtain for the first time a complete and structured overview of the asset consumption necessary for the production of services. Cost accounting can do this, as it does not - as the cameralistic does - calculate the changes in the amount of cash assets, but utilization of resources.

Costs, as is defined above, represent evaluated performance-related consumption of resources during a period of time. This definition describes the term „costs" with four characteristics (cf. Hummel/Männel 1990, 73ff.).

* First there must be a use of resources. In libraries, this is the use of human work, as well as the use of operating resources - information technology, office furniture, rooms, etc.

* Then the consumption of resources has to be caused by the production of services; that means only those uses of resources are regarded as costs that happen in the pursuance of typical operating goals. For instance, the typical operating goal of a vehicle repair shop is the maintenance and repair of automobiles; the main goal of university libraries is the provision of information for the university. If library rooms are occasionally used for seminar meetings, the costs of managing them are to be charged pro rata to the faculty using them, and not to the library.

* Furthermore, the use of resources has to be evaluated; that means to be expressed in units of money.

* Finally, the use of resources is always shown with reference to a chosen accounting period (month, quarter, academic term, year).During the implementation phase of the cost accounting, this will usually be an annual account.

The compilation of asset consumption related to the accounting period causes essential deviations from the cameralistic accounts. For instance, the cameralistic considers investment measures only in the year that the acquired capital asset - e.g. a security system for books - was paid for. That security system, however, is not used up in the fiscal year of its acquisition. On the contrary, it is of use to the library for a succession of following accounting periods, in which it is gradually worn out. The service oriented use of resources spreads itself over several years; and correspondingly the asset consumption must be evaluated in every utilization period. This periodization of the expenditure made in the year of acquisition is effected in form of calculated depreciation against the operating funds of the library. In other words, it distributes the expenditure made for the capital asset to the whole useful life of the asset. In calculated depreciation, costs exist that in the accounting period do not lead to expenditure of the same amount.

A further case of costs differing from expenditure, a case essential to the practice of library cost accounting, is given by the approach of calculated retirement pay for civil servants. There the present use of resources and the corresponding costs to be considered, only lead to payment in future periods. The examples show that an evaluation of the library oriented on actual use of resources leads to significantly different results than the accounts of cameralistic.

Cost transparency achieved by the complete overview of the asset consumption is the basis for a second goal, the calculation of the library product, specified as to quantity and quality. This goal will gain increasing importance in the context of the progressing financial autonomy of universities. In the course of budget globalization, the narrow restrictions of the traditional item-economy are falling away. In the future, universities will have to work with an all-inclusive budget, upon the use of which they can decide for the most part independently and unregulated. That process of decentralization of resource management presently determines the university politics of all states of the German Federal Republic, whereby the speed of the development as well as the extent of the granted financial scope clearly varies from state to state (cf. Behrens 1996, Chap. IV; Brinckmann 1998, 146ff.). The university internal distribution of funds to faculties and central units will concentrate on the output oriented budgeting. In such models, the university management makes agreements with the respective organizational units about the service products, differentiated by quantity and quality, that are to be produced within a planning period. The core of such agreements is the ascertainment of the costs of the respective products, on the basis of which then the budget allocated to the operational units for autonomous management is calculated (cf. Künzel/Nickel/Zechlin 1998). Cost accounting as an instrument of performance oriented budget assessment is here filling the vacuum of coordination that arises from the discontinuation of the close meshed item structure of traditional budget plans: The input steerage is replaced by an output oriented financing.

Libraries will also have to present cost calculations of their service products and to base their demands for funds thereon (cf. Stäglich 1995; Wätjen 1994). At the same time, the concept for output oriented budgeting gives broader scope to library management. If the budgets for staff, for investments, and for operating expenditure are coverable, and if additionally the option exists of building capital reserves on a larger scale out of all budgets, the library can substantially influence the structure of the costs it causes. That is especially true when - as it is for instance already practiced at State and University Library of Bremen - the detailed financing of a position chart is also waived in favor of an all-inclusive staff budget. The granting of financial autonomy thus lastingly facilitates the availability of given funds; however at the same time, the new decision making power might lead to conflicts in the libraries:

- Should the gains made by rationalizing be used for more staff or for necessary investments?

- Should the library react on cuts by waiving new recruitment and preferment of staff, or by canceling journals?

Here again cost analysis of the available alternatives of action contributes to an objective discussion.

If the costs of the library's services are calculated on the basis of the topical condition, the available resources, existing organizational and business processes; the calculated „prices" do not give evidence concerning the economic efficiency of the service production, in other words the extent to which the ascertained costs are reasonable in comparison with the produced service. Here comparison with other institutions can help to evaluated efficiency. This so-called benchmarking, the comparison of the own service costs with those of other institutions, is often regarded in the literature as the most important instrument for cost management of public institutions (cf. i.e. Eichhorn/ Bräunig 1997, 107ff.). Since these are not commercially oriented, and their services are not offered on the market, excessive prime costs and correspondingly calculated „prices" cannot be „punished" by a decline in sales. Cost comparison should create a competition surrogate. Benchmarks, that is service processes exemplarily mastered organizationally and economically, can give an incentive for improving the own work processes.

Economic comparisons between university libraries are, however, made difficult by the fact that though their mission - to supply the university with information - is clearly defined, the extent and quality of the provision of services for the most part is not specified closer. As service processes and products of university libraries are not sufficiently standardized the comparison of the prime costs by itself is not very informative. For instance, one library could give the offer of electronic delivery service a high priority and provide qualified staff and expensive technology for it, whereas a comparison library might consider that service an additional service and run it with the least possible use of resources. If benchmarking shows that the costs for one document delivered in both libraries are about the same and also near the expense ratio of other libraries, the conclusion suggests itself that a reason does not exist to improve their cost situation. Actually, however, the equality of the cost levels can conceal manifest inefficiencies of the service production in the library that gives the analyzed service only a subordinate importance in their „product portfolio", and consequently should also show clearly lower costs per product. Thus an informative benchmarking requires cost analysis of the service processes running „behind" the library services that are necessary for the product. Not the cost per unit, for instance, of one online delivery is primarily relevant for steerage, but the cost of the activities necessary for its processing, such as „fetching and scanning the document", „processing complaints", „monitoring payment", etc. Only that kind of cost information presents the possibility of following the production process of library services through all steps of the course of business and hereby discloses how the costs accumulate along the way. Benchmarking can then direct itself - flanked by quality ratios especially regarding processing - at the identification and analysis of the factors causatively determining the costs. For instance, the decision to classify electronic delivery service as an additional service can lead to employing exclusively support staff. The analysis of all the work processes involved would then perhaps show that, in comparison to other libraries, a clearly higher manpower need hereby arises for coordinating tasks (detailed rosters, etc.) and for the processing of complaints (due to a higher error rate), which for its part effects a cost increase of the services. Benchmarking would in that manner ascertain the actual cost driving processes and at the same time point out the way of changing the cost situation by deliberate intervention into the service structure.

A further application of cost accounting is the ascertainment of the costs additionally incurred with the introduction or the expansion of services. The calculation of decision dependent costs is significant for libraries, above all for the establishment of electronic services. Developing a virtual library fundamentally changes the service profile, the operational procedure and the organizational structure. The tasks newly arising here are primarily related to providing, offering, and preparing digital information - be it metadata or full text publications - for use. At the same time, work processes focused on the traditional collection building lose importance. The economical evaluation of the alternative courses of action for each given case requires here the calculation of the so-called *relevant costs*, those resource usages that arise by the decision for offering a certain service and consequently are to be considered in the cost related evaluation of that decision. Those kinds of functional accounting needs detailed and differentiated cost data, since they are fundamentally designed as direct costing. If a library, for instance, decides to join an online delivery consortium, the relevant costs of the decision are the costs of the hardware and software to be purchased, as well as the costs of the staff capacity needed for the order processing, however not the costs of the already existing net- and PC-infrastructure or building and management costs. The same goes for the ascertainment of gain from rationalization measures achieved by the reduction of traditional services - e.g. the conventional inter-library loans. Only those resources, which in the case of a reduction become available for other purposes, the ones directly allocable to the considered product, are decision and cost relevant.

The ascertainment of relevant costs will also gain importance in the remuneration calculation of fees. Here the assessment of payment to be made for the electronic delivery services used stands in the foreground. In this area, which is especially important for the profile of academic libraries, there is a tendency to depart from the principle that public services - especially in the education sector - are to be paid by the general public through taxes. The trend is in favor of provision of services financed more by the user. There are two ways for the libraries to calculate fees for electronic document delivery and other costed services:

• Either, with the goal of a full cost recovery, the costs directly connected with the performance of the service, plus the proportional ascertained costs for overhead, infrastructure, and management are charged.

• Or, should that procedure lead to rates that have a prohibitive effect on the use of the services offered, at least the reimbursement of the costs directly allocable to the service will be required.

Here again, the costs directly connected to the product are to be differentiated from those caused by the library's general readiness to operate.

A further application field of cost accounting often referred to in the present discussion about administrative reforms is the support of decisions about own production or outsourcing of public service (cf. Stößel 1998). For libraries, the possibility of outsourcing suggests itself mainly for the routine operations of media processing (order administration, processing, etc.), as well as for project tasks (retro conversion, implementation of IT-systems, etc.). The necessary cost analysis has to reach into the microstructure of the processes concerned in order to provide significant comparative data regarding the offers of private service providers. Thus for instance, a project carried out at the Bavarian State Library that tested outsourcing acquisition procedures, required the calculation of costs for processes like „unpacking the delivery and controlling its completeness" or „checking the factual and calculative correctness of receipts" (cf. Griebel 1999). In the cases where the own production is too expensive and outside purchasing seems advantageous, it must be kept in mind that outsourcing measures can only lead to a reduction of costs when the affected capacities can be reduced or at least shifted. Especially in the area of staff costs, short term relief by outsourcing is not to be expected due to extensive dismissal protection regulations.

So far cost accounting was considered as to the provision of decision supporting information. The active steerage of the library's cost structures with the goal of a sustained economical increase goes further than that, and is the task of the actual cost management. It requires the deliberate influencing of the factors of the service process decisive for cost occurrence. Costs are only symptoms of the causatively effective cost determining factors (cf. Franz/Kajüter 1997, 11). Costs arise when resources (staff, equipment, space, etc.) are provided. Resources in turn are consumed in work processes, which on their part serve the production of services. This relationship, which has already been explained in short in chapter 1.1, means that interventions in cost management cannot be directly applied to the costs, but always to the factors determining them. Since the library's service processes represent the resource using and thereby cost driving factors, *continual process optimization* is the essential starting point for increasing economic efficiency.

Looking at the work structures of academic libraries, it becomes clear that significant rationalization potentials could lie there. The marked functional specialization of the staff, as well as the organizational style strongly based on the division of labor effects that, as a rule, different stations work together on generating a product. Thus for instance at University and Regional Library of Münster, four cost areas are involved in the provision and execution of electronic document delivery(information, loans, stacks, IT-department). Looked at from the perspective of the total process, the interfaces between the involved organizational units often appear as arbitrary interruptions of the work chain with the result of process loops, superfluous rework and revisions. Because cost accounting assesses the resource usage being attributed to the concerned activities, the cost effects accompanying a process optimization can be calculated exactly. It becomes perceivable

- to what extent improvements of the process organization lead to a reduction of resource needs,

- to what extent the gained resources help to increase the quantity of performance or can be shifted to the bottle-neck areas,

- and to what degree the cost situation of the service analyzed changes thereby.

Besides the continual improvement of the process structures determining the resource need, the *cost management of capacity* and the *management of cost flexibilization* constitute the relevant instruments for the active cost management of service institutions and therefore also of libraries (cf. Friedl 1997, 122ff.; Haiber/Dunker 1995, 481ff.). University library costs are mostly capacity costs, which means they arise in connection with the building and maintenance of service potentials, above all by the provision of staff, space, and equipment. Capacity costs occur, for instance, by the provision of staff for cataloging and inquiries, by the provision of IT-systems, of user work places, and of space for the stacks. A certain performance ability of the library is defined by the resources held available. Thus for instance, a loan department equipped with a certain number of staff and issue desks, is able to carry out two million loan operations per year. This productive capacity exists independent of whether and to what degree it is used. Its costs are consequently not influenced by changes in the volume of services rendered. If only 1.5 million loans are effected in one year, that does not mean a change in the amount of salaries to be paid or in the depreciation to be stated. Capacity costs are thus costs that occur independently of the intensity of use of the services offered. They are therefore referred to as the costs of operational readiness, or simply standby costs. On the other side the proportion of costs directly service related, in other words the costs that automatically vary with the degree of utilization of the capacity held available, is in libraries, as in service institutions in general, rather small. Examples of that kind of service related or variable costs are costs for labeling and binding, which directly vary with the number of books procured, or the costs for shipping material and postage, which are directly dependent upon the amount of documents sent through delivery services. Due to that cost structure, measures that limit themselves to look only at the quantity of product units do not result in much. For instance, the provision of user friendly retrieval software and search engines may lead to a reduction of reference and inquiry cases. The hereby realizable cost reduction potential, however, remains unused as long as staff, equipment and tasks of the service area „information center" remain untouched; on the contrary, with a lessened performance quantum, the „unit costs" of a reference answer even rise. Cost guiding measures must be primarily aimed at influencing the standby costs, that means aimed at the adaptation of the service potential to the actual service demand, by deliberate intervention into the capacities held available.

Since the costs of the capacities held available are independent of the actual volume of service, they have the character of fixed costs. They can only be influenced by enlarging or cutting of the service potential held available, but not by changes in the degree of utilization of that potential. The extent to which disposition of the operational readiness is possible essentially depends upon the commitment period of the fixed costs. So for instance, the purchase of a reader printer causes cost for the whole depreciation period, whereas a leasing contract, if need be, can be cancelled at short notice. The cost management of capacity, accordingly, has to be flanked with a management of cost flexibilization aimed at raising the cost controllability or cost responsiveness, e.g. by giving preference to limited as opposed to unlimited employment. Moreover, because of the high proportion of fixed costs, cost analysis of library and of general university services is only limitedly usable for steerage measures effective ad hoc - such as cost reduction programs. Its task lies primarily in the support of middle- and long-term decisions, especially in the areas of restructuring tailored to the demand and of reallocating the built-up service potentials.

For this purpose, cost information is necessary that puts the costs of the resources provided in relationship to the costs of the resources actually used (cf. Cooper/Kaplan 1995). If it is known to what degree each service potential held available is really used, superfluous capacities or capacity needs can be recognized and adaptation measures can be taken. The traditional cost type and cost center accounting reveals only the costs of the resource provision. It shows what the total costs arising for the maintenance of the library's service potential are composed of (staff, material costs, operating costs, calculatory costs, etc.) and how they are distributed to the library's departments and functional centers. The provided service potential determines at the same time the amount of available service processes. Thus in the above mentioned example, the chosen outfitting of the loan department with staff capacity and equipment determines that two million loan operations can be carried out yearly. The costs of the resources used on the other side depend upon how often the available service processes are de facto used in each accounting period. They relate to the actual demand for the processes made available through the build-up of service potentials. The juxtaposition of the costs of the service processes held ready and the costs of the service processes demanded then shows the degree of utilization of the potentials held and makes idle-capacity costs and idle time visible. The surplus resource offer is in principle available for reduction or reallocation, which in turn leads to an improvement of the considered service area. That kind of analysis of the relationship of used-capacity costs to idle-capacity costs should furthermore always be considered in benchmarking projects. If the performance comparisons are, as is presently the normal case, merely related to the costs of the provision of services, possible existing overcapacities and the corresponding idle-capacity costs are hidden, in other words - corresponding with Schmalenbachs familiar dictum - slovenliness is compared with slovenliness.

In library cost accounting, the structure of the accounting and stirring systems is significantly determined by the fact that libraries are not manufacturing units - but service institutions. The intangibility of the produced product, which makes clear identification of the cost unit difficult, as well as the high proportion of fixed costs, which hinders the short-term use of known cost cutting potentials, have already been mentioned. Economic publications show that service institutions, when compared with industrial companies, show a low state of development in regards to cost analysis: „It is to be regarded", states Corsten in his standard work on service management, „that cost accounting and furthermore the whole accountancy show a dominant orientation on the industrial production conditions, and that only in recent times questions about service companies have received more attention" (Corsten 1997, 257). Especially in regards to the intangibility of the service production, it is emphasized that traditional accounting systems can hardly deliver cost information relevant to decisions and steerage. „In pure service companies, ... up until now the cost accounting has not gone beyond an undifferentiated allocation of costs to the cost centers on the basis of a full absorption costing. The costs of the activities, that is to say of the services, disappear into the cost centers like into a ‚black hole' and a provision of information for planning, decision, and control purposes is only partially possible" (Serfling/Jeiter 1995, 321). In the following, the service profile of university libraries will be characterized in more detail in reference to the economical term „services". It will be shown how the library's „global product", provision of information for the university, can be diversified in form of a product catalog and be calculated in a cost accounting way. In the chapter after that, the activity based costing will be described in detail as the calculation instrument specifically suited for service institutions.

1.3 Services as a Cost Accounting Object

Up to now, there is no commonly accepted definition of the term „services" in business administration, with the help of which the variety of the existing kinds of service can plainly be characterized and clearly delineated from the provision of goods. Due to the „high complexity and heterogeneousness of the examined object ‚services'" (Meffert/Bruhn 1997, 30), only the typical characteristics can be shown, through which services are usually characterized. In business administration, a phase model developing in three steps, is recommended for the description of the fundamental characteristics of services (cf. Hilke 1989, 10ff.):

- In the *potential phase*, capabilities and readiness are built up to perform services for those requesting them.

- In the *process phase*, service processes are provided to the satisfy the request for service.

- In the *result phase*, the creation of benefit for the requester takes shape as an effect of the service process.

According to this model, service is to be understood as a sequence: Its phases are built upon each other, and only in their wholeness do they allow a complete description of the examined object. The potential phase is hereby related to the procedure of building up those accounting capabilities necessary to be able to bring about a certain result. This happens by a combination of production factors adequate for the service goal, in other words staff, machines, buildings, information technology, etc. Thus the library has to

- provide an adequate amount of staff capacity with the appropriate qualification,

- build up a collection in keeping with the subject profile of the university,

- offer good search instruments, and

- create a technological infrastructure that allows a comprehensive and up-to-date access to various collections of data.

In short, the potential phase comprises the build-up and maintenance of those factors necessary for making use of services.

By the employment of the service potential, the performance of the service is then effected in the process phase. This phase is formally characterized by the fact that the service readiness concretizes itself onto an external factor, that means a factor lying outside of the service supplier's disposition (cf. Meffert 1997, 65). That factor is either the recipient of the service himself or an object brought by him into the service process. The former is, for instance, the case when medical treatment is received, the latter, when a person takes his car to the repair shop. In libraries the external factor is the user or his any given information need. Accordingly, it is intrinsic to the process phase that the service supplier can only begin the service performance when the demander brings a process triggering element, to be more precise, the external factor, into the service process. Only if there is an information need on the part of the user can a reference transaction be carried out, media prepared for use, documents handed over or delivered, and networked data accessed. Hereby it does not make a difference whether the user is dependant on the intervention of library staff to cover his information need (e.g. by going to the information desk), or whether he uses library services autonomously (e.g. by looking in the open access stock on site). For library services it is essential that the provided utilization potential meets with the external information need that is brought in. The external factor represents a necessary condition for services (cf. Hilke 1989, 12; Corsten 1997, 125).

In the result phase, the effect of the executed service processes finally concretizes itself for the requester in form of a benefit resulting from using the service. For the library user this effect consists in the fact that he receives the desired information or the desired document at the desired point in time. The perceived benefit that the service „library" gives consists in the timely availability of information tailored to suit the needs. In the result phase no more activity is done on the provider's side.

The description of the three service phases shows that intangibility is an intrinsic characteristic of services. Services change conditions or restore them (examples: janitorial services, hair cutting, business consulting), but they do not transfer any objects. That is where they differentiate themselves categorically from manufacturing companies, which produce and market material goods, and from commercial companies, which buy and sell such goods. The intangibility of the services does not mean, however, that no kind of physical objects are put to use in the service performance. So the repair of a car requires in certain cases the replacement of the brake shoes, but the service result perceived by the customer is the restored operativeness of the vehicle; and this is without a doubt an intangible good (cf. Hilke 1989, 14f.). Likewise material information carriers are processed, when documents are scanned/copied, electronically/postally sent off, and in certain cases printed out at the delivery site, while a document is delivered. However, the service is not the document itself, but its punctual provision at the recipient's work place. Because of this intangibility and the necessary inclusion of an external factor services are as a general rule not able to be produced in advance for stock. That means that services are not able to balance out fluctuations in demand by stock piling. Consequently, possibilities to economize at a steady level while demand constantly changes are very limited. .The fact that services defy stock-piling underlines the significance of capacity cost management for service companies. As explained in chapter 1.2, standby costs dominate in university libraries. In other words the costs that arise in the framework of the build-up and maintenance of the offered service potential. A large portion of the total costs are determined in the potential phase of the service performance, when quantitative and qualitative dimensions of the services offered are decided on. The shaping of the potential factors - e.g. decisions about designing capacities for a peak or an average demand - plays a decisive roll in library cost management (cf. Friedl 1997, 118f.).

At this point the objection could be raised that the service characteristics mentioned above do not apply to that library service which at the moment is still the most important, namely the local collection of books and journals. It could be argued that those are doubtlessly of a material nature, which can be confirmed by there storability in stacks. Analogous to the above mentioned example of document delivery, it is true that the library's service does not consist in the media procured and kept by it, but in the provision of the possibility of their use. Similarly it is true for a car rental that it is not the fleet of cars parked on the company's parking lot, but rather the surrender of the use of the car calculated daily that makes up the service of the loaner. Accordingly the possibilities of use cannot be stockpiled in order to be called up in times of stronger demand. They only exist for each of the considered time periods and expire when they have not been taken advantage of. This can best be illustrated by means of a concrete case. A procured textbook, for instance, has been part of the collection for four years. Assuming that the loan period is for two months, there are a total of 24 possibilities of usage. Since the book is barely asked for during the vacations, 10 chances of usage are not taken advantage of. Each one of those chances are only available during the period of time defined by the lending period and expire if no borrower (external factor!) shows up. It is obviously impossible to „stockpile" those 10 chances of usage in order to retrieve them during the semester when the demand clearly goes beyond the remaining offer of 12 options of use. Time is irrelevant. It makes no difference if a document is available for 4, 30, 50 or even 100 years. If in-house-use rather than loans is taken as appropriate form of usage, the opening hours of the library are to be used as measure of the available chances of usage instead of the loan period. In regards to the provision of networked digital information, the described facts are also evident: Here, for instance, the number of licenses obtained for a certain contract period defines the extent of the total usage potentials kept on hand.

From the perspective of the service recipient, the services of a university library can be described as a timely availability of information suitable to the needs. It takes shape as a perceived creation of benefit in the result phase of the service performance. From the perspective of the service provider, the same service is characterized as providing access to information and allowing for its use. In this context it does not matter whether that happens in the form of loans, document delivery systems, or access to digital data. In the potential phase, the necessary operational readiness is build up, e.g. through

- the procurement and processing of media,

- the installation and administration of a loan system,

- the provision of hardware and software for document delivery services,

- the provision of user work stations and teaching rooms, etc.

In the process phase, the services are performed to satisfy the demand by using the established operational readiness. Books are issued, documents delivered, searches executed, user instruction courses held, reference questions answered, events organized, etc. To characterize more closely the service product produced by the combined effects of potential and process phase, it is, first of all, to be emphasized that the term „process phase" does not cover only those processes running in that phase. The chosen terms should exclusively emphasize that it is not the mere provision of potentials, but only their concretization on an external factor during the procedure of service that makes up the service. But also the services performed in the potential phase are essentially of a procedural nature, to be more precise, processes of the build-up and the maintenance of service abilities (cf. Niemand 1996, 76ff.): Media are acquired and made accessible, internet sources processed, user PCs installed, user instructions prepared, upgrades in the network installed, schedules for the use of rooms made, restoration work carried out, networks administrated, third-party funding attracted, air-conditioning controlled, etc. The activities taking place during the potential phase of the service performance could be called structural processes, whereas the activities carried out in the process phase represent so-called handling processes (cf. Hermann 1966, 178ff.). Structural processes are in a means-end-relationship with the handling processes. Their services are, under certain circumstances, of benefit to an arbitrary number of handling processes, for instance the once-only processing of media for a multitude of loan operations.

The „global product" of academic libraries, the provision of usage possibilities of information resources can in the first step be subdivided into structural processes on the one hand and handling processes on the other hand. The former erect and maintain the library's service readiness and define thereby the potential phase of the service performance. The latter employ the built-up service ability for the creation of benefit for the demander and make up the process phase of the service. In the result phase no processes run any more on the part of the library. However, the user's evaluation of whether and to what extent the performed activities have brought about the desired benefit, depends decisively on the quality and quantity of the service processes. In a second step, the structural and handling processes can then be further subdivided vertically as well as horizontally. The vertical differentiation is predetermined by the framework given in the library organigram, namely department heads, departments, and functional centers. From the cost accounting point of view, the library's cost centers are being dealt with here. An example for the cost centers, the services of which are allocated to the potential phase, is the acquisition department. The activities performed here, such as „bibliographic checking of books to be ordered", „carrying out orders", „sending reminders to suppliers", „accessioning media", „transferring money for the payment of bills", etc., are clearly structural processes. They serve the build-up of stock and thus the maintenance of the library's service readiness. In contrast to this the loan department as cost center clearly belongs to the process phase. The operations running here, such as „handling loans and returns", „issuing library cards", „sending out overdue notices", „collecting fees" etc., serve the processing of the loan operations including the direct involvement of external factors, of the user, to be more precise. Besides such cost centers clearly classed with one of the two phases of service performance, mixed forms also exist that involve structural as well as handling processes. An obvious example for this is the cost center „subject librarians". The services here, like „selecting the media to order", „subject indexing," and „processing internet sources", serve the build-up of service potential. Other tasks, however, such as providing subject information for users or holding user education courses use these potentials to satisfy the user's need for information.

The horizontal differentiation of the library's process structure is effected in a functional-center-overlapping way. The processes that are of interest out of the different cost centers are chained together to form a comprehensive service bundle. In this way the work steps that according to procedural logic belonging together, yet that are spread out over several cost centers, can be consolidated into coherent service modules. The service performance can thus be illustrated as a continual process, where numerous partial services of different organizational units are interlocked. From a cost accounting perspective the advantage of this cross-functional geared operation lies in the fact that the question, which process elements are connected together and, as the case may be, are revealed as „product", exclusively depends on the given calculation purpose pursued. Sub-processes such as „stacks" (fetching and reshelving original document), „delivery" (scanning a document, generating a status report, etc.), „accounting office" (invoicing, following up invoices), and „IT-department" (administering DOD-station), must be brought together in order to calculate the charges for electronic document delivery services. The service „delivering documents via document delivery systems" represents a complete process made up of a multitude of sub-processes.

Because of the fact that potential phase and process phase, respectively structural processes and handling processes, are integral parts of a service there is a danger of depicting the library's products from the start only on a very high aggregation level of the involved partial services. The successive splitting up of academic libraries' core business - the provision of the possibility of usage of information resources - into a multitude of partial processes suggests itself here as an alternative. These are connected in a logical way, namely vertically, reflecting the library's structural organization, as well as horizontally, illustrating its operational organization, As soon as these partial processes are evaluated in regards to the resources used by them and to the cost allocated to them, they make up in their entirety a data-pool capable of being flexibly evaluated. This allows the calculation of arbitrary performance structures in the library. It solely depends on the accounting objective, which partial services are hereby aggregated and which are differentially depicted. Against the background of this process model, the formulation of elaborate product catalogs, as e.g. for public libraries (cf. Pröhl/Windau 1997, 19f.), primarily obtains a heuristic function: That kind of catalog makes up a valuable orientational framework that points to possible ways of condensing the partial processes down to more comprehensive service modules. However, it should not be understood as a binding standard that fixes the function of cost accounting one-sidedly to the provision of highly aggregated ratios for external needs for information. This is especially true for the conception of a product plan for academic libraries as presented in chapter 4.1.

Services always come into existence through the combined effects of potential, process, and result phases. That is the reason many services, that make up autonomous products from the library's point of view, will inevitably appear from the service recipient's perspective as partial services at the most. When looking at the product „media distribution", then this would be described by the processes „booking a loan" „reshelving the media", „sending a reminder", "collecting fees", "executing a courier delivery", etc. For example, the service description in one of the product catalogs produced by Municipal and University Library Frankfurt, defines the product "distribution" exactly in this sense (cf. Naumann 1998, 308). De facto, however, it is simply the matter of the handling processes being a necessary partial element of a service that is to be described from the users point of view as "a temporally limited transfer of the right of usage of the medium". In short, the service "media distribution" does not consist in taking a book out of the stacks and handing it over the issue desk but rather in the student's using the book for a certain period of time instead of buying it. In order to make this possible, the potential phase of this service is also indispensable, namely the acquisition, processing, and storing of the media by the library. Under certain circumstances, these structural processes are, as was shown, of benefit to an arbitrary number of handling processes, and indeed not only in the context of local circulation, but also of inter-library loans and reference use.

In regards to cost accounting it is, therefore, extraordinarily difficult to justly set off costs that arise in the potential phase against those that are allocated to the process phase. As was explained in chapter 1.2, the costs of the potential phase is a matter of capacity costs and thereby fixed costs. Since they are brought about by the build-up and maintenance of service readiness, they are not directly related to the service units to be rendered (cf. Bertsch 1991, 46). Taking into account to possibility of allocating them to the generated product units - a document delivery, a reference transaction, a loan, etc. -, they are hence to be characterized as overhead costs. These are the costs that jointly occur for several cost accounting objects. Consequently, those objects cannot be directly allocated, but only with the help of clearing ratios and apportionment formulas. In traditional cost accounting systems the unit costs ordinarily serve as the allocation base, in other words the costs directly allocable to the cost accounting object. These are primarily a matter of material costs and of wages occurring directly in the framework of production, especially piece wages, which are proportional to performance. The material overheads, e.g. for logistics and purchasing, are then burdened with percentage surcharges on the basis of the cost of direct material. The production overheads, for instance, for operations management and for quality control, are set off against the product on the basis of the prime costs (for the allocation procedures possible here see Kilger 1992, 188ff.). In libraries, as generally in service companies, the capacity costs and thus the overhead costs, as described, dominate, whereas the proportions of the unit costs directly allocable to the generated service unit is at least significantly small. So, for instance, the unit cost of products like „user education" and „reference service" can be limited to the paper- and print costs of the information material. These residual factors are not only unsuitable as a surcharge basis, but also are not in a cause-effect-relationship with the overhead costs being offset. One causal relationship, however, let us say between the amount of material and the acquisition expense, has to be assumed, if overhead costs are to be assigned to the products on the basis of cost units. For instance, the staff and technology costs occurring for the offer of electronic document delivery evidently do not vary with the costs for postage, shipping material, and long distance data transfer that occur as unit costs in the context of order processing.

In reaction to the lacking suitability of traditional accounting procedures for the analysis of service areas having intensive fixed costs as well as overhead costs, the *activity based costing* was developed. It waives the undifferentiated formula assignments and allocations in favor of a cost analytical penetration of the actions and activities running in the area of overhead costs. The operating procedures evaluated in regards to capacity need and occurrence of costs can then be assigned according to their degree of being used by products. Hereby it is decisive for the purpose of service calculation that the illustration of service procedures is done in the form of a process hierarchy that is based on the continual chaining of partial processes and thus allows the almost arbitrarily differentiated or, as the case may be, aggregated expense ratios. The basic ideas and methodical concept of this approach are represented in the following chapter, which thereby builds the bridge to a concrete construction of library cost accounting.

1.4 The Concept of Activity Based Costing

The operating procedures necessary for the production of a service use resources and thereby cause costs. Activity based costing aims at the evaluation of resource consumption for every partial step of the provision of services. Bringing the partial steps, evaluated in regards to costs and capacity requirement, together then offers a differentiated picture of cost emergence for all stages in the process of adding value. Because the service is split up into the sub-processes it is made up of, measures taken for the improvement of the cost efficiency can intervene directly and accurately into the process structure of whichever performance structure is analyzed. Activity Based Costing was developed in the U.S.A. in the 1980s, with the goal of a cost accounting penetration of the growing overhead proportion in modern companies (cf. Miller/Vollmann 1985; Johnson/Kaplan 1987; Cooper/Kaplan 1988). In

Germany, the reception of Activity Based Costing began in 1989 with the contribution „Prozeßkostenrechnung: Der neue Weg zu mehr Kostentransparenz und wirkungsvolleren Unternehmensstrategien" („Activity based costing: The new way to more cost transparency and more effective company strategies") by Horváth and Mayer (Horváth/Mayer 1989; cf. Horváth/Mayer 1993). The approach developed by Horváth and Mayer differs from the American Activity Based Costing especially in that it incorporates the cost center accounting developed very differentiated in Germany (cf. Gaiser 1998, 68f.). Activity based costing, which quickly found broad recognition in company practice, reacts to changed production conditions in highly flexible and highly automated production systems. These are characterized by a preponderance of steering, controlling, planning, and coordinating activities in relation to the actual production process. Economically, these activities are assigned to the so-called indirect service areas, in other words spheres of activity such as research and development, acquisition, production preparation, production steerage, quality control, logistics, etc. In regards to cost accounting, it is a matter of areas of overhead costs. That means the costs occurring in them - in contrast to production salaries and material costs - cannot be directly allocated to the manufactured products.

The costs of indirect service areas are traditionally burdened onto the manufactured product unit by means of percentage surcharges on the cost unit prime costs. However, that procedure ignores, as it was shown in the previous chapter, the conditions actually causing the emergence of overhead costs. In this way, for instance, the costs of acquisition, checking the material, and inventory controls do not vary depending on the material value, by which they are traditionally allocated to the product, but rather depending on the kind and number of the procedures concerning order, control, and storage (cf. Fischer 1997, 156). Given a dominating overhead proportion of the total cost, the traditional surcharge procedure leads to clear distortions in the calculation of product and price. For instance, the production of complex product varieties requires the activities of the indirect service area, let us say for inventory planning, production steerage, and quality control, to an especially high degree. If the costs of the indirect service areas are offset against undifferentiated percentage costing rates, all products are assigned the same overhead rate regardless of whether they are standard pieces or variants. The variant, which is expensive in regards to the whole production procedure, is thus burdened too little and correspondingly offered on the market too cheaply, whereas the less expensive standard piece is evaluated with too highly calculated prime costs and, as the case may be - if the price level is correspondingly calculated

-, has to fight against a sales problem. It goes without saying that serious wrong decisions could result, for instance in the streamlining of a range of products.

The activity based costing tries to avoid these deficiencies by assigning the costs arising in the indirect service area directly to the resource consuming activity in that area. The subject-matter of cost analysis is thus processes like „processing offers", „executing order contracts", „managing inventory", „introducing new articles", „paying delivery bills", etc. The cost values allocated to those service processes are ascertained on the basis of whatever resources are required, especially staff capacity. The quotient coming out of the costs of a process and the activity quantity then leads to the costs of a one-time execution of that process, the so-called process cost unit rate. By means of this cost unit rate, the costs of indirect service areas can then be offset in a way that does justice to causality, that means according to the quantitative degree the processes are used by the product.

The following greatly simplified example should make this procedure transparent: At the cost center *purchasing*, processes A: „procuring the components for standard products" and B: „procuring the components for custom-made variants" are carried out. In an accounting period, costs of 20,000 Deutschmark (DM) are ascertained for process A and 3,000 DM for process B. The number of procurement transactions within this period comes to 160 for process A, and 20 for process B, resulting in a process cost unit rate of 125 DM for A, and 150 DM for B. A standard product X with a annual production volume of 400 requires 50 procurement transactions A. Consequently, each product unit is to be burdened with 15.60 DM procurement costs (50 x 125 / 400). A custom-made variant product Y with an annual volume of 5, demands 10 procurement transactions B, resulting in procurement costs of 300 DM (10 x 150 / 5) to be shown for each product unit. By showing in each given case specific (thus doing justice to causality) process cost unit rates for standard products as well as for variants, the process oriented calculation leads to a clearly different burdening of the manufactured product unit. As opposed to that, the conventional calculation for surcharges would have allotted the total occurring overhead costs of 23,000 DM for the procurement transactions with a percentage surcharge on the basis of the material unit costs, in other words, on the basis of the material value of all of the procured components, to the products. Given an assumed material value of 80,000 DM for all of the company products, each product unit would be to be burdened with a surcharge of 28.8% onto its material unit costs (23,000 / 80,000 x 100). Assuming that 110 DM material unit costs occur per standard piece X and 160 DM per variant piece Y, 31,70 DM would be shown for X, and 46.10 DM for Y. The material overheads to be shown for the manufacturing of custom-made product variants would thus have been calculated clearly too low (46.00 DM as opposed to 300 DM on the basis of process costs), whereas the standard product would have been burdened too greatly (31.70 DM as opposed to 15.60 DM on the basis of process costs). This in turn could have lead to wrong decisions, let us say in regards to the expansion of the production of the variant as a presumed profit earner.

The activities running in the indirect service areas of manufacturing companies correspond structurally with the operating procedures and courses of business in service companies, especially in the area of banks, insurance, and in the public sector. Here as well as there, administrational routine operations predominate with a high degree of formalization. Operational processing serves as an example, in other words standardized and repetitive operations like „processing offers", „executing orders", „processing bills", „administrating customer data", etc. Since the same service conditions generally exist in service companies as in the indirect areas in industrial companies, the activity based costing can be applied to all of the processes of service production. The cost unit „service" is, as was explained in the previous chapter, to be described as a process sequence of partial services linked together in a logical way according to the matter, and can therefore be depicted completely by activity based costing. If, for instance, the costs of a electronic document delivery order are to be calculated, the costs occurring for task execution, bill processing, etc, are to be compiled and then divided by the amount of orders completed within the period in consideration. Due to the process character of the cost accounting object „service", the activity based costing can thus be considered as the prevailing instrument for the assessment and steerage of service costs: „Whereas activity based costing in industrial companies can only be looked upon as a supplement to the existing cost accounting, it is, due to the identity of cost units and process, adequate as a sole cost accounting system in service companies." (Serfling/Jeiter 1995, 322; cf. Horváth/Mayer 1993; Zimmermann 1992). The calculation steps of activity based costing will be presented in the following to the extent it is necessary for the comprehension of the method concept of this approach, whereas the practical details of the accounting construction will be described in part 4 (cf. also the summarized depictions by Olshagen 1991; Müller 1998).

Step 1: Task Analysis on the Level of Cost Units
   To begin with, the executed sub-processes in all of the cost centers are ascertained. A sub-process is defined in the terminology of activity based cost-

ing as an operation in relation to earlier and later operations, that is delimited according to subject matter and time, with - as a rule - measurable resource input and output. Thus in the cost center *subject librarians* the sub-processes: „selecting media to order", „processing media sent on approval", „subject indexing", „holding user instruction courses", among other things can be differentiated. Most of the time a sub-process in turn consists of several activities. The sub-process „ordering media" in the acquisition department, for instance, consists of the activities „examining the order data", „selecting the supplier", and „placing the order". A sub-process is always an operation within a cost center.

Step 2: Ascertaining the Process Times and the Costs
The proportion of the total staff capacity for the considered cost center occurring per sub-process is determined by means of time logs or time estimates. Manpower requirements for sub-processes is expressed in employee years. According to the proportion of the staff capacity the annual total costs of the cost center are then distributed over the sub-processes. That is how the costs for sub-processes for the analyzed accounting period are obtained. Setting off the cost center costs in proportion to the required employee capacity represents the standard procedure of activity based costing (cf. Mayer 1998, 15). It is based on the premise that staff costs represent the dominant cost type, and thus all other cost types - operating costs, building costs, etc. - can be distributed over the sub-processes in the same proportion as the staff costs (cf. Kajüter 1997, 221). For instance, at University and Regional Library Münster, three of the total seventeen employee years for the cost center *subject librarians* are spent on the sub-process „subject indexing" (not including the use of external data); that is 17.6% of the available staff capacity. Accordingly, the sub-process is burdened with 17.6% of the cost center costs of 2,711,500 DM, resulting in costs of 477,200 DM. At the library in Münster, an employee year - including deductions for sick leave and vacation time and other time debits - corresponds to 1,476 annual manhours. Accordingly, 4,428 manhours are expended annually for making the material accessible. All of the numerical values mentioned here and in what follows are real data, whereby the accounting period, fiscal year 1997, serves as an example.

Step 3: Identifying the Cost Driver
For sub-processes, benchmark figures are established for the determination of the performance. In the terminology of activity based costing these measuring units are called cost drivers. An example will explain what is meant by cost driver. The process „ordering media" performed in the cost center ac-

quisition by purchase is always carried out when an order entry exists. The receipt of an order in this cost center triggers off activities connected with the process of ordering media such as pre-order bibliographic searching, filling out purchase order forms, etc.. The execution of these activities consumes resources (working time, material, etc.) and thus causes costs. The measuring unit „number of orders", therefore, represents the cost determinant, the cost driver, of the process „ordering media". Further examples of cost drivers are: number of reference questions, number of loans, number of database updates. A cost driver is, in other words, the measuring unit for the extent that resources are being used by the operating procedure. The literal meaning of the term cost driver makes that especially clear. The number of orders is, so to speak, the „driving force behind the costs" of the process „ordering media". Every new incoming order triggers off the process and causes the costs connected with its execution. Hence the cost driver is at the same time a benchmark figure for determining the process output. The number of the processed order entries defines the activity quantity of the operating procedure. The cost driver consequently represents the decisive measurement for the quantification of the processes, both in regards to the level of cost, as well as in regards to their activity quantity. At University and Regional Library Münster, for instance, the process „subject indexing" covered 14,635 indexed documents.

Step 4: Calculating the Process Cost Rates and Processing Time
The process cost rate is calculated by the division of the cost of whichever sub-process is being considered by the its activity quantity, i.e. the average cost of a single execution of the sub-process. Analogously, the quotient of staff capacity and activity quantity results in the processing time, in other words, the average time required for a single execution of the sub-process. For the sub-process „subject indexing", the result on the basis of the depicted cost and process time is a process cost rate of 32.60 DM and an average processing time of 18 minutes per indexed title. The described steps of the sub-process analysis lead, as a result, to a process model of the library that delivers the following ratios (cf. Ceynowa/Finkeißen 1998, 471ff.):

• Staff capacity of sub-processes, expressed in employee years;

• Costs of the sub-processes in the accounting period considered;

• Activity quantities of the sub-processes, expressed in the quantity structure of the cost driver;

- Process cost rates of the sub-processes, expressed as the quotient of cost and activity quantity;

- Processing time of the sub-processes, expressed as the quotient of staff capacity and activity quantity.

The sub-processes, evaluated in relation to cost and capacity, represent the components of the library's services, which are, as a rule, designed in a cost center overlapping way. Service relationships like these, coming into existence by connecting sub-processes, are called main processes. A main process is a chain of sub-processes, belonging factually together, from one or more cost centers. Main processes thus do not represent a new „kind" of process, but simply connect a chain of sub-processes to form a superordinate process structure. They describe the services and thereby the cost units of the library (cf. Niemand/Rassat 1997, 48). By introducing main processes, the activity based costing completes the decisive step to an examination of work sequences covering both overlapping interfaces and functions. This becomes particularly clear when looking at the role of sub-processes in the accounting construction. These build, so to speak, the joint between the cost center costs, which in each cost center are allocated to the sub-processes, and the main processes designed to be cost unit overlapping (cf. Mayer 1998, 8). They thus build a bridge between a cost analysis designed to be construction oriented, and a process oriented view of cost occurrence. On the basis of the constructed process model, the costing of the main processes is done by linking the involved sub-processes together. It does not matter in which cost center the sub-processes were performed. This is exemplified by *figure 1* for the main process „electronic document delivery", in the processing of which usually at least four cost centers are involved: the stacks (sub-process „bringing forth the original document"), the functional centers responsible for processing the delivery (sub-processes „scanning the document", „generating the status report"), the billing station (sub-processes „processing the bill", „controlling the inpayment") and the IT-department (sub-process „administering the document order delivery system"). Bringing the evaluated sub-processes together then automatically results in the expended staff capacity for each considered main process, as well as its cost (cf. Kajüter, 1997, 212). By determining the cost drivers of the main process, in this example the number of orders, the processing time and the process cost rates can be calculated on the level of the main process.

Through the interplay of the sub-processes and main processes, the library service performance becomes illustratable in form of a process hierarchy. For each given analysis purpose, this hierarchy can be expanded downward, e.g. through the application of activities, the sequence of which sub-processes are made up of; as well as upward, for instance through the application of comprehensive business processes. Thus, the mentioned sub-process „administering the document order delivery system" can be divided up into the activities of „insuring operational readiness", „processing error occurrence", „implementing updates", etc.; whereas on the other hand, the main process „electronic document delivery" together with the conventional inter-library loans, local loans, reference services, etc. can be brought together to form a business process.

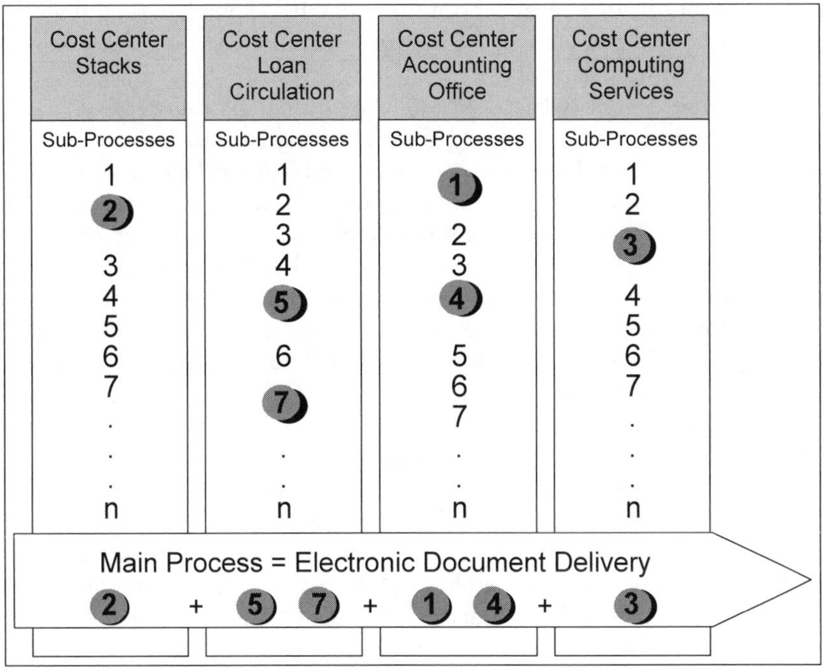

Cost Center Stacks	Cost Center Loan Circulation	Cost Center Accounting Office	Cost Center Computing Services
Sub-Processes	Sub-Processes	Sub-Processes	Sub-Processes
1	1	**(1)**	1
(2)	2		2
	3	2	**(3)**
3	4	3	
4	**(5)**	**(4)**	4
5			5
6	6	5	6
7		6	7
	(7)	7	
.			.
.	.	.	.
.	.	.	.
n	n	n	n

Main Process = Electronic Document Delivery

(2) + **(5) (7)** + **(1) (4)** + **(3)**

Fig. 1: From Sub-Processes to Main Processes

In this context it is clear that every differentiation „downward" is primarily motivated by internal steerage goals, whereas consolidations „upward" mostly serve external needs for information, let us say in the framework of university annual reports. The constructed process hierarchy allows the structured illustration of the total operational procedures of the library in a process oriented perspective free of overlaps. It leads to a cost model constructed according to the modular building-block system: In principle, when the sub-processes of all cost centers are evaluated in regards to staff capacity, cost driver volume, cost, and process cost rates, every library service can be illustrated according to its cost structures by connecting the involved sub-processes together. In particular, the cost of services that are „spread" over a multitude of cost centers can be extracted exactly out of the total cost of the library - such as the internet based information services or the tasks of a deposit library. For this is the sub-process structure has to be adapted correspondingly. Thus the sub-process „subject indexing" rendered in the cost center *subject librarians* has to be further sub-divided (legal deposit monographs ..., purchased monographs ..., electronic media ..., etc.), if, for instance, the library wants to ascertain the standby cost of legal deposits.

Furthermore, activity based costing allows a fair allocation of services to the library's products for classical overhead cost centers such as *administration and management* and *IT*. Here as well a correspondingly worked out sub-process division is needed, as was shown in the context of the IT sub-processes to be assigned to the electronic delivery services. In the cost accounting for University and Regional Library Münster, for instance, the sub-process „administrating student assistants", which causes an annual cost of 27,700 DM, is to be found in the cost center *general administration*. The administrative cost student assistant is calculated by using the cost driver of the sub-process - the number of student assistants occupied in the library. Given 70 student assistants (1997), the process cost rates amounts to 396 DM. On the basis of that, the service areas employing the student assistants can then be burdened with the cost thereof according to the quantitative degree the sub-process is used. In the cost center *textbook collection*, for example, 9 student assistants are listed, consequently the cost center receives - process cost rates multiplied by the process quantity - 3,564 DM administrative costs for student assistants allotted. These examples also show that for the identification and delimitation of processes no uniform procedure can be given. On the contrary, it depends exclusively on the specific problem and accounting objective as to which and how many sub-processes and main processes are to be differentiated. The modeling and subdivision of the processes thus represents the actual creative act of the accounting procedure (cf. Staud 1999, 10f.).

In regards to the steerage aspects, the most important characteristic of the process model that is summarily represented in *figure 2* lies in the cost center overlapping layout of the main processes, or as the case may be, services. It creates the possibility of bringing the individual sub-processes together, depending on the analysis goal, into different main processes. Activity based costing is equipped with a high evaluation flexibility and corresponds to the demands placed at the outset for a data storage usable for manifold accounting purposes. In particular, it offers the chance of rethinking the structure of the library in regard to the organization of its operations. This no longer makes its appearance as a static entity made up of hierarchically divided areas of task and function, but rather as a dynamic structure in which the process sequences consolidate to increasingly complex operational relationships.

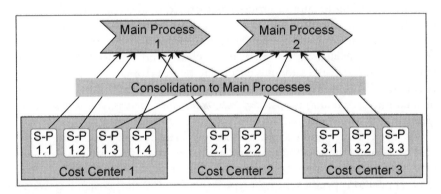

Fig. 2: Construction of a Process Model

Departments and positions are not much more than „process fragments" in this model, in other words mere through stations of a function overlapping process flow: The hierarchy of departments and tasks is - at least tendentiously - replaced by the hierarchy of process levels (comp Hammer/Champy 1996, 43f.). In addition, the analysis of the interplay of sub-processes and main processes immediately shows the organizational deficiencies that are based on an insufficient process orientation of the library. This is where the essential causes of deficient efficiency of service performance lie and thus represent the decisive points of intervention for cost management, the strategy of which is explained in part 5. The following chapters begin by describing the details of the construction of the library cost accounting divided according to accounting steps, cost type accounting, cost center accounting, and the cost unit accounting - which is designed as activity based costing.

2 Cost Type Accounting

2.1 Construction and Division of Cost Type Accounting

Cost type accounting has the task of categorizing and depicting all costs that arise in the framework of service production within one accounting period. The categorization is according to the type of employed production factors, and used resources, respectively. It answers the question: „Which costs have arisen?". The breakdown of all of cost types occurring in the company ordered according to subject group is performed by the cost type plan. This is to be constructed according to the criteria of completeness, unequivocalness, and absence of overlapping: All resources consumed in the service process are to be evaluated; these are to be clearly and unmistakably defined, whereby again their assessment is ensured to be free from overlapping (cf. Coenenberg 1997, 67). The cost type scheme of a university library can be subdivided into five main groups: *staff costs, media costs, running administrative costs, operating costs, calculatory depreciations.*

As a rule, three subdivision levels are sufficient for the structuring of the cost types of the library: the cost type group, the cost type, and the cost sub-type. Assignment is done according to a three digit numerical key, whereby the first position specifies the cost type group (i.e. 100 staff costs), the second the cost type (110 staff costs, civil servant), and the third the cost sub-type (111 staff costs, civil servant, academics). The cost type accounting informs about the cost structure of the library, for instance about the relationship of media costs to staff costs. Beyond that, changes in the cost structure become visible by comparing several accounting periods. In this way, the cost effect, for instance, of a far-reaching coverage ability of staff expenditures, material expenditures, and investments can be made transparent and brought into relationship with the library's development planning. Furthermore, the cost type accounting shows the proportion that fixed and variable costs make up of the total cost of the library. It thereby makes the possibilities and limitations of a short-term influence on the cost situation evident. As explained in chapter 1.2, the cost type accounting is directed exclusively at the ordered and complete depiction of the costs of the provided resources. It thus does not say anything about to what degree those resources are actually needed, in other words to what extent possible idle-capacity cost occur. It neither enables an evaluation of the economical utilization of those resources.

2.2   Assessment of the Staff costs

Since staff costs represent the largest pool of cost of a university library, this cost type group should be sub classified in detail. The type of employment relationship is suggested as a criteria for differentiation. Salaried employees and civil servants can be subdivided into academic and non-academic staff. The following division of the cost type group *100 staff costs* is suggested:

100	STAFF COSTS
110	*staff costs, civil servant*
111	staff costs, civil servant, academics
112	staff costs, civil servant, non-academics
113	calculatory retirement pay
114	fringe benefits
120	*staff costs, salaried employees*
121	staff costs, salaried employees, academics
122	staff costs, salaried employees, non-academics
130	*staff costs, worker*
140	*staff costs, assistants*
141	staff costs, student assistants
142	staff costs, student assistants (post-grad)
150	*staff costs, work creation program*
160	*staff costs, projects*
170	*other staff cost* (further subdivided if need be)
180	*administrative overheads surcharge*

Staff costs can be calculated on the basis of the actual expenditure occurring or on the basis of average rates. Several problems occur when using real costs: Due to the protection of data privacy, the use of real costs proves to be difficult, and it can lead to wrong information and undesired steering effects. For instance, the application of real costs distorts the inter-temporal comparison of several accounting periods. Cost increases or -reductions can not only be caused by increases or decreases in the workforce, but also by the changes in marital status and in the age structure of the employees. Therefore, changes in the efficiency of staff placement, i.e. through staff cuts or reallocation of capacities, are in certain cases hidden if operating with real data. Moreover, the application of actual costs could also lead to a preference towards younger and childless applicants, since real cost cutting effects can be obtained in this way (cf. Kuhnert/Leszczensky 1998, 17f.).

Hence, average rates should be used for the calculation of staff costs, whereby different assessment bases come into question. For instance, the staff cost rates for civil servants, salaried employees, and wage earners released by governmental departments can be used. Yet, these are, as a rule, indiscriminately ascertained beyond all government agencies. They do not show any specification according to administrative or organizational units and thereby in certain cases do not do justice to the personnel structure of the university area. Therefore, average costs specific to universities are to be preferred. As a first measure those expense ratios can be considered that are used for the calculation of monthly savings due to vacant positions in the budget globalization (e.g. as with Paff 1998, 221). The values applied here, however, are also a rough estimate since they normally leave several classification steps untouched.

Thus, the application of state-wide average rates specific to universities for every level of the position chart is more realistic. For the state North Rhein-Westfalia (NRW), they have been ascertained in the model experiment concerning university cost accounting, which was presented in chapter 1.1 (cf. Kuhnert/Leszczensky 1998, 19). These values, which are quoted in *figure 3* „Average Staff Expenditure of the Universities in the State NRW in Budget Year 1997", were drawn upon for the assessment of the staff costs in the project libraries. *Figure 4* shows supplementary the values for the state's polytechnics, whereby, however, only the data for 1995 are on hand. The annually required adaptations to the tariff could either be undertaken on the basis of each given pay settlement or simplified by a percentage surcharge based on a rough estimate. The project libraries chose the second way, using a value of 2% as a basis. Since North Rhein-Westfalia has a differentiated and widely expanded university landscape with traditional universities as well as newly established universities, the NRW-average rates are sufficiently representative and can also be used outside NRW. Therefore, inasmuch as own calculations are missing, these rates should always be given preference over undifferentiated rough-average values. The high degree of correspondence of the average rates to reality is shown by means of a comparison with the real data carried through for the staff costs of University and Regional Library of Münster. The actual costs of the employees with civil servant status lie at only 1.8%, those of the salaried employees at 2.1% lower than the staff expenditures calculated on the basis of average rates. The values mentioned in *figures 3* and *4* encompass all components of remuneration effective in the payment. In other words, besides the employer's contribution to social security and the complementary insurance, it also includes the bonuses for vacation and Christmas (cf. Kuhnert/Leszczensky 1998, 18).

Average Staff Expenditure of Universities of the State NRW in Budget Year 1997					
Civil Servants		Salaried Employees		Workers	
Classification	Expenditure	Classification	Expenditure	Classification	Expenditure
A5	39.713,06	IX b	47.856,29	1	42.511,83
A6	42.452,85	IX a	58.288,70	2	52.693,66
A7	47.006,46	VIII eD	57.782,51	2a	53.369,14
A8	52.545,26	VIII	53.339,78	3	54.826,95
A9 Z	60.476,70	VII	61.670,92	3a	60.536,69
A9	50.888,41	VI b	66.018,21	4	57.471,10
A10	61.903,19	V c	71.265,33	4a	62.752,06
A11	71.274,53	V b mD	80.609,09	5	58.639,17
A12	81.487,53	V b	73.682,08	5a	66.510,43
A13 gD	90.526,83	V a	63.567,34	6	62.341,28
A13	84.669,86	IV b	84.650,98	6a	67.653,10
A14	100.034,65	IV a	95.110,53	7	67.349,46
A15	112.379,37	III	106.083,68	7a	73.781,04
A16	124.740,18	II b gD	95.861,61	8	71.709,01
B2	141.012,10	II a gD	120.242,17	8a	76.980,68
B3	142.183,96	II b	92.235,92	9	77.029,56
B4	148.582,80	II a	94.389,03		
B5	163.016,64	I b	123.025,38		
B6	172.769,64	I a	132.551,25		
		I	146.909,23		

Fig. 3: Average Staff Expenditure of Universities

Calculatory retirement pays as well as the payment of allowances should be included in the calculation for civil servants - corresponding to the inclusion of the employer's contribution to social security and the contemplary insurance for the salaried employees. *Calculatory depreciations* are the representation of an actual resource consumption that leads to payments in future periods. For the sake of a complete cost assessment, their placement into the cost accounting is thus indispensable. In the project universities, the calculatory retirement pays were calculated with a surcharge of 30% of the staff costs of employees with a civil servant status. This percentage rate is customarily taken as a basis in the federation's and states' economic analyses. For the assessment of allowance costs, an average value of 3,143 DM annually per employee with a civil servant status has been taken. This value was calculated by the Finance Department of North Rhein-Westfalia.

Average Staff Expenditure of Polytechnics of the State NRW in Budget Year 1995					
Civil Servants		Salaried Employees		Workers	
Classification	Expenditure	Classification	Expenditure	Classification	Expenditure
A5	38.772,36	IX b	51.368,18	1	59.078,22
A6	42.502,79	IX a	60.815,21	2	51.318,41
A7	43.538,14	VIII eD	55.234,56	2a	51.387,78
A8	53.680,78	VIII	53.827,40	3	52.967,15
A9 Z	60.471,43	VII	58.711,82	3a	57.238,56
A9	48.678,36	VI b	63.338,31	4	52.975,71
A10	58.105,29	V c	68.111,09	4a	58.262,11
A11	67.616,78	V b mD	78.300,26	5	54.825,00
A12	80.156,81	V b	67.534,63	5a	62.084,43
A13 gD	90.623,69	V a	58.163,52	6	62.943,29
A13	79.750,82	IV b	74.764,17	6a	62.816,93
A14	96.029,79	IV a	85.927,14	7	63.144,21
A15	110.291,44	III	97.847,95	7a	70.725,46
A16	124.378,42	II a gD	114.777,48	8	66.785,10
		II a	105.727,19	8a	71.499,89
		I b	123.660,20	9	73.049,23
		I a	129.847,31		

Fig. 4: Average Staff Expenditures of Polytechnics

For the calculation of *staff costs* for assistants, the scales of remuneration made available by the university administration should be drawn upon. These scales presently show a remuneration rate of 15.68 DM pro student assistant hour and 24,82 DM pro student assistant (post-grad). When changes occur in the social security law, these values are to be updated accordingly.

Administrative overheads cover the costs for the services the library achieves by external administrative units. For the library, administrative overheads encompass both the services of university (university cash department, allowance office, etc.) as well as non-university (center for cooperative cataloging, etc.) administrative units. This cost type calculated with a 10% surcharge on the gross staff costs shown in the regular budget. It is understood as a provisional equivalent for future models for billing services (KGSt 1998, 14f.). If the service centers providing service are for their part equipped with a cost accounting, they can load the costs of their products onto the administrative units receiving the service. This leads to corresponding valuations in the cost type accounting of the service recipients. To obtain structures similar to the market new models are thought about. For instance, statewide services from a consortium could be budgeted directly to the receiving universities. In using such a concept, libraries would become „buyers" of service offers from competing cooperation centers, with a corresponding cost burden being placed on the account. This client/supplier relationship could also be established for the calculation and transfer of employee remuneration, e.g. by contracting private accounting centers.

It is to be emphasized that the percentage rate of 10% as mentioned above is a relatively rough flat-rate value, which is, in addition, only regarding the administrative structure of a municipality. Corresponding calculations for the university area, however, do not exist. Using the percentage of 10% cannot lead to an exact calculation of the administrative overheads of the library. The calculated costs rather serve as a „memorandum item" showing that the library's services is dependent on manifold support services from external sources.

The ascertainment of the valuations for the cost type group *staff costs* doesn't require a big effort. It essentially consists of the evaluation of the library's position chart by means of the average rates for staff expenditures and is complimented by several constants for the assessment of calculatory retirement pays, allowances, etc. At the same time, a high proportion of the library's total costs are covered by this cost type group: The staff cost of the accounting period 1997 comprises, as an average of the three project libraries, 60% of the total costs.

2.3   Assessment of Media Costs

The cost type group *200 media costs* can be divided up in the following way. (According to the task profile and desired depth of information, further subdivisions can be undertaken.)

200	MEDIA COSTS
210	*scientific literature*
211	scientific literature: monographs
212	scientific literature: periodicals
220	*electronic media*
221	electronic media: acquisitions
222	electronic media: licenses

223   electronic media: costs per access
230   *other media*
240   *binding*
250   *preservation*
251   preservation: restoration
252   preservation: filming
253   preservation: other measures

The ascertainment of the media costs does not present a problem for libraries. The valuations, can usually easily and quickly be taken from in-house data sources, especially from the acquisitions department. Except for the costs for electronic media and for preservation, the International library statistic can also be fallen back upon.

The cost type *preservation* comprises external orders as well as the costs of the material necessary for preservation. Occasionally there is a discussion about whether the costs of information carriers acquired during an accounting period can be offset against calculatory depreciations. Funk favors this way (Funk 1975, 57ff.). He assumes a depreciation period of ten years for the literature of the domain of science. The idea of depreciating the library's collection is underpinned with the reference to the material depreciation through wear and tear and the antiquation of the knowledge accumulated in the material. (Benkert 1998, 28). This argumentation, however, holds true for academic libraries only in the area of textbooks and some of the natural-academic and technical information. Even here, the ascertainment of a consensual depreciation period might meet great difficulties (cf. Umstätter/Rehm/Dorogi 1982, 51). In all of the humanistic and sociological subjects, the ascertainment of an „intellectual date of expiration" for academic information is impossible. A one-dimensional research process, which definitively outdates the demands for older knowledge through new knowledge does not exist in these subjects. Furthermore, rare and historical collections, which in the course of time experience a substantial increase in value, cannot at all be assessed by the concept of collection depreciations.

These difficulties can be avoided, when - as is suggested in this book - the cost type group *media* is exclusively burdened with financial means expended within the accounting period. (Costs in this costs type group arise through media acquisition, license obtainment, and database accesses.) This procedure is also to be preferred in regards to steering aspects. The decisive cost driver of the work process is the acquisitions, and not the existing collection. On the average for three project libraries, the cost type group *media costs* took up 26%

of the total costs. The future development of the cost levels for this group will primarily be determined by two aspects.

- To what extent are printed media displaced by electronic information carriers?

- To what degree replaces the pay per view for digital information acquisition or license obtainment.

With pay per view, the media costs occur relative to the operation, that means, only when a concrete demand arises. Potential idle-capacity costs caused by purchase and licenses can not arise. Thus, out of the perspective of cost accounting, the transition to a virtual library would be supported without restriction. However, the advantages of a broad offer of information resources kept on site remain disregarded.

2.4   Assessment of Running Administrative Costs

The cost type group *300 running administrative costs* represents a mixed group consisting of communication costs, costs for maintenance and repair, costs for low-value assets and business needs as well as a number of smaller items that are to be determined in each individual case. For the sake of high assessment accuracy, the following fine division of the groups was suggested to the project libraries. If need be, it can be greatly simplified by doing without the cost subtypes:

300	RUNNING ADMINISTRATIVE COSTS
310	*communication costs*
311	communication costs: telecommunication
312	communication costs: postage
313	communication costs: long distance data transfer
320	*costs for maintenance/repair*
321	maintenance/repair: building technology (incl. telecommunication equipment and LAN)
322	maintenance/repair: ADP-equipment and software care
323	maintenance/repair: other equipment, machines, furniture, etc.
330	*material costs*
331	material costs: equipment/outfitting under 800 DM (not ADP)
332	material costs: ADP-materials of consumption (incl. Hardware and Software under 800 DM)
333	material costs: business needs (office material, small articles, etc.)

340   copy costs
350   travel costs
360   cost for further education
370   other administrative costs

The ascertainment of the values of these cost types demands drawing upon heterogeneous, and oftentimes manually maintained data sources. The latter ones additionally often have to be obtained from service centers external to the library. The gathering of *telecommunication costs* can be done by falling back on bills showing the occurring costs either per connection or as a lump-sum for the whole library. In libraries that have their own mail room, the *postage costs* can easily be gathered on the basis of the annual statement for outgoing letters, packages, book shipments, etc. Hereby, the postage directly repaid by the user (e.g. the reservation-notices) should be dealt with as a transitory item and correspondingly not be included in the calculation. If a central postal department supports a whole university, an estimation procedure has to be applied- inasmuch as no partial accounting per service center exists. The library departments substantially affected (loan department, doctoral dissertation unit, etc.) should estimate the approximate number of annual outgoing shipments of the library on the basis of a random sample analysis. The cost proportion to be burdened to the library is then corresponding to the proportion that the library's shipments make up of the central postal department's total outgoing mail. It is to be applied to the total postage costs of the university.

Regarding *long distance data transfer*, it occurs that the university computer center often does not have any information about the distribution of costs to individual user groups and organizational units. An acceptable approximated value can be attained by the following formula: $[A/B]*C$ with

A   total long distance data transfer costs of a period arising for the university

B   total number of connections to the internet

C   number of connections to the internet that the library makes.
    (A and B are provided by the computer center)

The *maintenance and repair costs* can be taken from two sources: a) the cost statistics for the use of the building provided by the university administration and b) databases maintained within the library for the management of materials costs. These, however, are often limited to a listing of orders for maintenance, repair, and care; and each entry has to be assigned to a cost subtype individually.

In the cost type *administrative costs*, the costs of all material and objects that are used up in the period of their acquisition are considered. This includes the business needs of the library, like office material (pencils, order forms, shipping materials, etc.) DP-materials of consumption (diskettes, cartridges for the copy machines, etc.) and small items (screws, keys, etc.). These things, are usually kept in an office material store room, and the date of purchase and the date of consumption are mostly close together. Discrepancies between expenditure and consumption could happen by materials being paid and put into store at the end of one period, and then being used in the following period. Those discrepancies can therefore be neglected as insignificant (cf. Kuhnert/ Leszczensky 1998, 27f.). Furthermore, some commodities are booked for the cost type *administrative costs*, are indeed permanently employed in the library. This is done if they have such a small value, that for simplicity's sake their offsetting by means of depreciations can be done without. Inadmitted asset are entirely cost effective in the period they are acquired, i.e. they are treated as if they get completely used up in this period (so-called „immediate depreciation", cf. Hummel/Männel 1990, 172). Customarily, all goods the values of which does not exceed 800 DM (excel. VAT) are hereby considered to be of minor value. This value limit is taken from the stipulation of the income tax law for the calculation of depreciations (EStG § 6, paragraph 2). Since parameters of the tax law are not obligatory for the purposes of cost accounting, other values can in principle be used, for instance, stocktaking limits given by university administration. Due to a uniform procedure required especially for inter-company comparisons, it seems, however, advisable to use the value limit of 800 DM commonly used in cost accounting. Low value assets are, for instance, trolleys, shredders, blackboards, chairs, office printers. The assessment of resource consumption entered in the cost type *administrative costs* is, as a rule, done using in-house data sources for material management.

The *copy costs* include the rent for the copy machines as well as the bill for the copies made. Copy machines owned by the library, on the other hand, are to be assessed in the cost type group *calculatory depreciations*, if they exceed the value of 800 DM. The costs for the copy paper is then to be entered in *administrative costs*. The cost of copy machines managed exclusively by a third party and just placed in the rooms of the library, are not to be assessed. Special calculations regarding the costs for room and energy occurring for this equipment should not be done, due to the insignificance of these costs. The copy machine costs can usually be taken from data sources maintained within the library. The same goes for *travel costs* and *costs for further education*, as well as for other running costs, like vehicle maintenance, fees, and dues.

As the average of the three project library, the cost type group *running administrative costs* takes up only 3% of the total costs. The ascertainment of the cost occurring in this group, however, causes a considerable ascertainment effort due to the scattered and unstructured data basis. For the sake of a pragmatic procedure, the application of the known 80/20-rule is recommended. According to the rule, 80% of the result can be obtained with 20% of the effort, whereas conversely, the remaining 20% result accuracy requires 80% of the effort (cf. Koch 1998). In applying this principle, libraries, for which a plausible average for this cost type is sufficient, should do the following: Taking the reference value of 3% ascertained in the project, the valuation for running administrative costs can be calculated implying a flat surcharge to the sum of the cost type groups 100, 200, 400, and 500. This is done according to the following formula: reference value = [(100/97-1) x the sum of the cost type 100, 200, 400, 500].

2.5 Assessment of the Operating Costs

The cost type group *400 operating costs* encompasses those expenditures of an accounting period that are made to ensure the operational readiness and usability of the library building. The following cost types are regarded as part of this group:

400	OPERATING COSTS
410	*energy costs*
411	energy costs: heating
412	energy costs: electricity
413	energy costs: water and sewage
420	*cleaning costs*
430	*costs for trash removal*
440	*costs for building security*
450	*costs for building maintenance*
460	*other operating costs*

Insomuch as the library is the sole user of a building, the values of this cost type group can be read from the cost statistics for the use of the building, which is made up annually by the university administration. Particularly faculty libraries as well as branch libraries of a library system, however, are mostly only co-users of buildings. Here, as a rule, a separate statement does not exist for every center using the building. The assessment of the proportion of the operating costs falling upon the library is then to be undertaken corresponding to the square meter proportion of the main usable floor space that the library takes up. The application of the allocation ratio „square meter proportion" can in certain cases hereby lead to an under- or overburdening of the library, let us say if it shares the building with an institute for semi-conductor physics. Therefore, if need be, the calculated values have to be corrected by a surcharge or deduction.

The cost type *costs for building maintenance* does not refer to the repair and maintenance of the building's technical equipment (cost type 321) or investments in the building's technology (cost type 510). It exclusively covers measures taken for maintenance of the operativeness of the building, e.g. measures taken for reconstruction and upkeep or for the repair of cases of damage (water penetration, etc.). As need be, assignment regulations are to be formulated for the avoidance of double counting. The cost type group *operating costs* makes up, on the average of the project libraries, 6% of the total costs.

2.6 The Assessment of Calculatory Depreciations

The costs of those assets that permanently serve the daily operation of business are assessed using calculatory depreciations. Besides the building, all assets with a value of over 800 DM (excl. VAT) are regarded as part of this group. Examples for assets of the library to be depreciated are: workstations, compact shelving units, reader printers, company vehicles, servers, library software, etc. As was explained in chapter 1.2, the expenditure and the costs for these assets diverge. While the expenditure occurs once on the date of purchase, the consumption of the goods and thereby the emergence of costs take place continually over many accounting periods. Correspondingly, the expenditure occurring once for the acquisition of a asset is to be allocated to the individual periods of its useful life. The calculation of the amount to be shown each period should be done according to the commonly used straight-line depreciation method (cf. Hummel/Männel 1990, 173).

According to this procedure, the expenditure made for the considered good is distributed evenly to the periods of its use. For this purpose, the investment outlay is divided by the number of periods of use. For instance, if a workstation for which a useful life of four years is assumed is purchased for 6000 DM in March of 1998, then 1500 DM annual depreciation are to be shown. Thus for the assessment of the written-down value, details are needed concerning the date of purchase, investment outlay, and the useful life of every asset used in the library. The available stock registers, however, as a rule provide only incomplete and insufficient information. In particular, details concerning the purchase price and the rated useful life are often missing. Hence, a stocktaking of the operating resources employed in the library is often indispensable. For every capital good with a unit value of over 800 DM (excl. VAT), this stocktaking needs to designate the year of acquisition, differentiated by the first or second half, the investment outlay, and the cost center making use of the asset. Inasmuch as these details are not able to be taken from the available data sources, then flat-rate values have to be worked with as need be. In the project libraries, for instance, the flat-rate investment outlay of 3,500 DM apiece for personal computers was taken as a basis.

For the assessment of useful life, standard depreciation rates released by the Federal Finance Department, are usually drawn upon in practice (cf. Hummel/Männel 1990, 172f.).

These indexes determine the minimum useful life for all common capital goods (for instance, 10 years for office furniture). However, looking at the factual time of use in the public sector, they mostly do not represent realistic values. Therefore, in the library's cost accounting, the „depreciation rates in the municipal administration" (KGSt 1999) should be primarily taken as a basis for determining the actual life. Being based on inter-municipally ascertained values drawn from past experience, the KGSt-indexes offer values specially adapted to public institutions. The time periods to be applied are hereby depicted in the form of intervals of use, in other words, by figures denoting a minimum and a maximum useful life. For instance, a useful life of 80 to 100 years is shown for office buildings, a useful life between 3 and 5 years for personal computers and workstations, and between 5 and 7 years for photocopy machines.

The period of use is to be fixed for each company within these comparative values corresponding to the special features given by the particular situation. For purposes of simplification, the average useful life is applied at University and Regional Library of Münster, for instance, 4 years for personal computers. Inasmuch as intercompany comparisons are strived towards, it is important that the libraries being compared choose uniform depreciation periods, regardless of which useful life was chosen.

Creating a stock register for the library does indeed require quite a bit of effort, however, it is a one time procedure. Afterwards, merely the running stocktaking of new acquisitions has to be done. Additionally, when the necessary data are compiled in the LIBRARYMANAGER, the depreciation expenses to be shown for each cost center are calculated automatically.

If libraries are not able to or do not want to take a inventory of their capital goods, they can limit themselves to the running compilation of the new acquisition beginning from the year of implementation of cost accounting. The resource consumption rated in the cost type group *calculatory depreciations* is then indeed clearly rated too low in the first years. However, its validity improves with every period the cost accounting is continued.

The cost type group *500 calculatory depreciations* can be subdivided in the following way:

500	CALCULATORY DEPRECIATIONS
510	*depreciations building/ building technology*
511	depreciations building/building technology: general library
512	depreciations building/building technology: faculty library A.
513	depreciations building/building technology: faculty library B. etc.
520	*depreciations non-real-estate fixed assets (over 800 DM)*
521	depreciations ADP-equipment
522	depreciations other equipment and machines
523	depreciations office and library furniture
524	depreciations company vehicles
530	*depreciations software (over 800 DM)*

The division of the cost type groups follows the commonly used differentiation between tangible (buildings, machines, etc) and intangible (software, patents, etc.) fixed assets. Further subdivision of the tangible fixed assets is done into movables and immovables (buildings and building connected technology). In the year of purchase, the full annual depreciation should be shown for movables acquired in the first half of the year, for movables acquired in the second half only half the annual depreciation should be shown. This procedure is automatically implemented in LIBRARYMANAGER. The acquisition date or, as the case may be, the stocktaking date should be considered as the starting point for the begin of use.

Another option in cost accounting is to take imputed interest of capital fixed in depreciable fixed assets into account. The application of imputed interest enables recording the interest for the capital that is needed to finance those assets ensuring service performance. This capital can either be borrowed so that actual interest payments have to be made or the financing can be done by owner's capital. Owner's capital is then no longer available for oth-

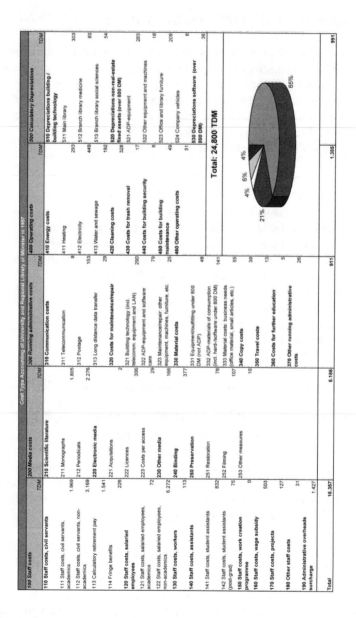

Fig. 5: Cost Type Accounting of University and Regional Library of Münster

er purposes, e.g. capital investments. In that case, interest earnings are lost that could have been obtained if the available capital had been invested in financial assets. The lost benefit of this alternative can be determined in cost accounting by the application of imputed interest on equity, which is also called opportunity costs (cf. Hummel/Männel 1990, 176).

For the assessment of imputed interest, a unique interest rate for owner's capital and borrowed capital is taken. Usually this is the interest obtainable for long-term capital market investments. A widely used procedure based on the interest rates of average values will be applied for calculating the value of the imputed interest (cf. Weber 1997, 124f.). For the whole useful life of an asset the average fixed capital serves as the basis for calculation. In regards to a straight-line depreciation, this is half of the written-down value. Thus for the workstation purchased for 6000 DM, 3000 DM would be fixed in the average of the total useful life. The amount of the imputed interest to be shown per each period is calculated by multiplying that result by the chosen interest rate. For instance, the calculated interest rate of 6% used by the Finance Department of North Rhein-Westfalia can be adopted. The annual imputed interest in the cost accounting for the workstation then amounts to 180 DM.

The question, however, arises as to whether considering imputed interest is meaningful for public institutions in the framework of decision-oriented cost accounting. Libraries, as non-profit organizations, do not pursue the objective of profit-minded capital direction. The funds that are assigned to them are to be employed in a earmarked way of fulfilling the library's tasks. Alternative uses, e.g. in the form of capital investments, do not exist. The calculation of imputed interest thus does not give any information directly relevant to steering. Their placement into the cost accounting would, at the most, function as a type of memorandum value that draws the attention to the fact that every expenditure burdens the funders with financing costs (Kuhnert/Leszczensky 1998, 24f.). The application of imputed interest has been done without in the cost accounting of the project libraries. Its calculation, however, can easily be carried out in LIBRARYMANAGER by entering the level of the interest rate. After designing the cost type group calculatory depreciations, cost type accounting is finished. On the average of the project libraries, this group claims 5% of the total costs of the library.

2.7 Concerning the Cost Structure of University Libraries

The results of the cost type accounting for University and Regional Library of Münster is presented in *figure 5* with the real data from the example period 1997. The cost structure of the library is characterized, as is typical for service providers, by the dominance of the cost factor „human work". In service companies in the private sector as well as in the public sector, the proportion of staff costs of more than 80% is generally taken as a basis (cf. Niemand/ Rassat 1997, 48). At University and Regional Library of Münster, it lies - if the media costs are not taken into consideration - at 83%. The distribution of the total costs of 24,800,000 DM to the cost type groups additionally show the high proportion of the capacity costs, in other words, the cost arising from the provision of staff, facilities, and space. They occur, as was explained in the previous chapters, independent of utilization, and thus represent fixed costs. Their amount is determined for a certain period of time by the decision of providing resources. This especially holds true for staff costs and the calculatory depreciations, which constitute 69% of the total costs (incl. media costs) of University and Regional Library of Münster. Most of all, long-term cost controls that can only be limitedly influenced by the library arise by hiring permanent employees, due to far-reaching dismissal protection regulations. In terms of cost technicalities, it is here a matter of so-called „sunken costs", which go back to decisions made in the past and hence, for the most part, avoid the managing grip. Consequently, the cost structure can only be changed within a long-term perspective, as is usual in the public sector. Working with global budgets opens up new opportunities for maneuvering, e.g. by being able to use personnel funds that become available from natural fluctuations for strengthening the media budget.

Capacity costs are only from the perspective of cost type accounting to be treated as fixed costs. If, however, the service products of the library is considered, i.e. the cost units, the bulk of the library's cost turns out to be controllable in the short-term. It can almost be arbitrarily adapted for each given goal. Every intervention into the available resources - e.g. the reallocation of employee capacities between main processes or the improved outfitting of a service area - precipitates, as part 5 will show in detail, in changes of the product costs. Those can for their part lead to adjusting the existing target figures and planning figures. The argument that the costs of the library (and in general, of the university) are fixed cost and thereby are mainly accessible to steering intervention in a middle- to long-term way, cannot be used as an objection against the need for an active cost management. It is, at the most, valid for the receipt level of cost types, and this is only true as long as the instruments for a financially autonomous fund management are not yet fully developed.

The assessment effort needed for the construction of the cost type accounting is essentially determined by the inadequate development of the necessary data pre-system. Foremost, the mostly insufficient care of central stocktaking databases, as well as the relatively imprecise material management are to be mentioned here. Thus, the relevant data, as a rule, cannot simply be called up, but have to first be made accessible. Hereby, setting up a duty of creating reports connected with a deadline receives a special significance.

In the ideal case of a developed university cost accounting, cameralistic data would be transferred to cost type accounting and provided to the operational units for utilization. This, however, will, in light of the de facto non-existence of cost accounting at universities (Kuhnert/Leszczensky 1997, 3), remain a future project for an indefinite period. Pilot projects show the future developments, particularly in regards to the effort of implementing the needed cost accounting software (cf. e.g. Ambrosy/Heise/Kirchhoff-Kestel/ Müller-Böling 1997). The work necessary for the construction of the cost type plan for the library, however, should not be overestimated. Particularly when the described procedural advice is accepted for the most part and, as need be, the running administrative costs are recorded as a flat-rate, the cost type accounting should be set up by a full-time employee within a month. Once the cost type plan has been set up, a clear reduction of the ascertainment effort is additionally to be reckoned with. In the continuation phase of the cost accounting, all of the relevant information sources are known and have been made accessible so that a well-founded data basis can be fallen back upon. Additionally, inasmuch as the compilation and maintenance of the data are done in LIBRARYMANAGER, all of the calculation routines built upon the values of the cost type accounting run automatically. To do this, the results of the cost type accounting are to be broken down to the cost centers of the library. The construction of the chart of functional accounts, as well as the method of offsetting the cost types against the cost centers will be described in the following.

3 Cost Center Accounting

3.1 Construction and Organization of the Chart of Functional Accounts

The cost center accounting answers the question: „Where do costs arise?" Its task is to assign costs to the places where the they arise. The construction of the cost centers can be undertaken from functional or spatial viewpoints or according to areas of responsibilities. For libraries, the structuring by functional areas seems useful. Thus, the chart of functional accounts matches for most part with the departmental and interdepartmental structure illustrated in the organigram. Two subdivisional levels ordinarily suffice: the cost center group and the cost center, whereby the latter, if need be, can be divided up further into subsections.

In the project libraries, the use of seven cost center groups worked well: *acquisition, cataloging, use, technical services, central services, special services, faculty/branch libraries.* Depending on the mission and size of the institutions, further subdivisions or bundling are to be undertaken if need be (e.g. in the case of integrated media processing). Due to the heterogeneous organizational structure of German university libraries, a reference and allocation list of all possible cost centers cannot be generated. Thus in the following, the chart of functional accounts for University and Regional Library of Münster is given as an example. Since the library is equipped with a broad service spectrum, its chart of functional accounts is quite suitable as a provisional framework of orientation. The chart comprises 35 cost centers, that are divided up as follows:

10 ACQUISITION
    11   subject librarians
    12   acquisitions department 1: monographs, electronic media, etc.
    13   acquisitions department 2: periodicals
    14   newspaper unit
    15   integrated processing of legal deposit media
    16   gift/exchange unit
    17   university publications unit

20 CATALOGING
    21   alphabetical catalog
    22   retrospective cataloging

23 editorial staff for serial catalog Münster
24 subject catalog

30 USE
31 local loans
32 inter-library lending
33.1 textbook collection, work area
33.2 textbook collection, user area
34.1 reading room, work area
34.2 reading room, user area
34.3 internet reading room
35.1 reference service work area
35.2 reference service user area
36.1 stacks work area
36.2 stacks user area
37 supervision services

40 TECHNICAL SERVICES
41 material purchasing and technical services
42 mail rooms
43 copy center
44 technical book processing
45 custodian services
46 circulation area and technology

50 CENTRAL SERVICES
51 general administration (incl. accounting office)
52 computing services
53 service center cataloging in departmental libraries (RZK)

60 SPECIAL SERVICES
61.1 manuscript department work area
61.2 manuscript department user area
62 center for historical collections in North-Rhine Westphalia
63 editorial staff, bibliography of North-Rhine Westphalia (NWB)
64 preservation
65 projects
66 hall for exhibitions and events

70 BRANCH LIBRARIES (BL)
71.1 social sciences BL work area
71.2 social sciences BL user area
72.1 medical BL work area
72.2 medical BL user area

Cost centers were divided into work area and user area, if staff workplaces and user area were directly related. For instance, the counters and provision areas of the reading room make up the cost center *34.1 reading room work area*, whereas the open access area and the reader space comprise the cost center *34.2 reading room user area*. This sub-division ensures the further settlements of the cost center costs against the sub-processes that are carried out in that center. As was shown in chapter 1.4, the entire cost center costs - including the building costs, administrative costs, etc. - are distributed to the sub-processes in proportion to the staff capacity taken up. Accordingly, for instance, if the sub-process „answering reference questions" performed in the cost center *reference service work area* uses up 30% of the total staff capacity available in that cost center, then 30% of the cost center's total costs are also to be assigned to this sub-process. This procedure is based on the assumption that the material costs and operating costs occurring in service companies are decisively determined by the number of employees (e.g. need for space, office material, PC-equipment). For that reason they can be offset against the sub-process in proportion to the employee capacity that it demands (cf. Becker 1997, 203).

In those cost centers that encompass both work- and user area, this relationship is only given, however, for the work areas. It is meaningful, for instance, to offset the electric costs of the employees' work places in the cost center *reference service work area* against the reference services that are rendered there. It would be absurd, however, if the energy costs occurring for the whole catalog room, or moreover for the whole open access area, were offset against these service processes. The processes would then be burdened with costs that they are not responsible for. The sub-division of the cost centers concerned into work area and user area prevents that kind of wrong assignment. The delimitation of the work areas from the user area inevitably means that the latter does not have any sub-processes and thereby does not bear any staff costs. The same goes for the cost centers *internet reading room* and *exhibition and event hall*, which also exclusively get material costs, e.g. for maintenance and repair, as well as for administrative cost and depreciations assigned. The sub-processes occurring for these cost centers, let us say the process „organizing exhibitions/events", are carried out in Münster in the cost centers *material purchasing and technical services* as well as *computing services*.

The cost center *circulation area and technology* needs to be explained. It encompasses the non-usable area (e.g. toilets, cleaning closets), the functional areas (all areas for housing the operational technology, e.g. the heating unit) and the circulation area (e.g. halls, stairs, shafts) of the library building. The amount of area of this cost center is thereby identical with the net floor space less the main usable space. The latter one in turn coincides with the sum of the amount of area of all of the other cost centers (cf. DIN 1998, 16f.). The cost center *circulation area and technology* includes only material- and administrative costs as well as depreciations.

As the procedure for the cost center group *70 branch libraries* exemplarily shows, it seems useful to list outsourced organizational units etc. as independent cost centers. Due to its mostly clear spectrum of tasks, as well as to the limited number of employees, it seems to be superfluous to again subdivide these sectional libraries for their part into cost centers. Their service structure can easily be represented on the sub-process level.

3.2 Offsetting the Cost Types against the Cost Centers

The offsetting of the values of the cost type accounting against the library's cost centers is done either by direct assignment or by using clearing ratios. The following ratios commonly used in the practice of cost accounting are used:

- The *staff ratio* describes the proportion that the staff capacity of a cost center makes up of the library's total staff capacity. The staff capacity of a cost center is hereby expressed in employee years. A employee year is the average annual amount of time that an employee is at the disposal of the company. Normed values should be taken as a basis for its calculation. In the project libraries, the following average numbers are used on the basis of a comparison extending over several years. 250 workdays are to be shown as the gross working time. 30 vacation days and 15 sick days are to be subtracted from that, which results in a net working time of 205 workdays. Given 38.5 working hours a week (= 7.7 hrs. per day), this corresponds to an annual working time of 1,578.5 hrs., or 94,710 min. This value comes very close to the annual working time of 94,000 minutes for civil servants and salaried employees in the municipal administration (KGSt 1995, 3). Since the pure working time is decisive for planning manpower requirements and staff placement, a flat-rate value for process allowance and personal needs allowance is additionally to be deducted from the net working time. Conferences, preparation time, etc. are to be regarded as part of the former; whereas, for instance, breaks and using the toilet are part of the latter. In the project libraries a flat-rate value of 30 min. per day was fixed for the assessment of these allowances; thus for 205 working days, 102.5 hrs. The net working time is reduced accordingly to 1,476 hrs. or 88,560 min. This is the value of an employee year. For student assistants, the total number of the hours student assistants are available in the cost center are regarded and then multiplied by the annual work weeks. Since every student assistant is entitled to four vacation weeks a year, 48 annual work weeks are to be taken as a basis. The employee capacity of a cost center that, for instance, encompasses 3 full-time employees, a half-day worker, one 75% employed employee, as well as three student assistants with 10, 15, and 19 working hours a week, results as follows: for the full-time employees 4,428 annual manhours (3 x 1.476 hrs.), for both of the part-time employees 1,845 annual manhours (0.5 x 1.476 hrs. + 0.75 x 1.476 hrs.), and for the three student assistants 2,112 annual manhours (44 hours a week x 48 weeks). The division of the sum of the annual hours (8,385 hrs.) by the value of an employee year (1,476 hrs.) gives as a result a staff capacity of 5.68 employee years for the cost center. If the library has a total of 160 employee years at their disposal, a capacity proportion of 3.6% is calculated for the cost center. Then if, for instance, the value of the cost type „business needs" of an assumed 50,000 DM is distributed to the library's cost centers by using the staff ratio, the considered cost center is to be assigned 3.6% of the costs, in other words 1,800 DM.

- The *square meter ratio* describes the proportion that the area of a cost center is of the total area of all cost centers. The total usable space coincides with the net floor space (main usable space + non-usable space + traffic space). The area value of the cost centers can as a rule be taken from the library's floor plans and ground plans.

- The *PC ratio* refers to the proportion that the PCs installed in the cost center make up of the total PC-inventory. The number of those devices can be taken from the inventory register, which - inasmuch as it is not already available - was constructed in the framework of the cost type accounting.

The following procedure suggests itself for the distribution of the individual cost types to the cost centers. The staff costs are directly assigned to the cost centers corresponding to each given employment relationship and the classification of the employees working in a cost center. Calculatory retirement pays are surcharged to the *staff costs* of the civil servants reported for the cost center according to the applied percentage value. The offsetting of the allowance costs is done in proportion to the number of civil servants employed in the cost centers. The administrative overheads allowance is to be place to the account of every cost center in relation to the staff costs listed in the regular budget (cost type 110 to 140).

The *media costs* are offset against the users areas - open access area, reading room, textbook collection, etc. - corresponding to the proportion of expenditures spent for each given area. The assignment of the funds expended for the user area and shelving area can, as a rule, be taken from the data banks maintained in the acquisitions department. If this is not possible, a qualified estimated value has to be worked with. The binding costs should be distributed according to the media costs to the user area. The costs for preservation, however, can be directly applied to the cost centers responsible for preserving and restoring measures. The distribution of the media costs to the user area is particularly necessary for the calculation of highly condensed ratios needed for external information. The costs for the basic provision for the students, for example, include the costs for processing and provision of textbook material plus the costs for space and the operating costs of the setup area of these media.

Within the cost type group *running administrative costs*, the telecommunication costs, inasmuch as they can be ascertained per connection, are assigned directly to the cost center. Inasmuch as lump-sum billing exists, they are to be offset by means of the staff ratio, in other words in proportion to the employee capacity of the cost centers. The distribution of the postage costs to the cost centers should be undertaken on the basis of a qualified estimate, preferably supported by a random sample analysis. In libraries that are supported by a mail-room external to the building, these calculations are already done in the cost type accounting step and can here be taken from it. The long distance data transfer costs can be offset just like the cost types 322 (maintenance/repair: ADP) and 332 (material costs: ADP) by using the pc ratio. The cost types 321 and 323 (maintenance/repair: building technology and maintenance/repair: other equipment, machines, furniture) can be distributed by using the square meter ratio, the material costs for low value assets and for business needs (cost types 331 and 333) by using the staff ratio. The staff ratio should likewise be used for all copy costs occurring in the service operation. Insomuch as the photocopy machines for the users are not ran by an external company, but rather by the library itself, their costs should be directly assigned to the user area that they are installed in. Travel costs and costs for further education can generally be allocated directly to the cost centers causing them. If possible, the staff ratio should be employed for the distribution of the other running administrative costs.

For the entire cost types of the group *operating costs*, the distribution to the library's cost centers is done by using the square meter ratio. This is also used for the allocation of the calculatory depreciations for the building and building related technology (cost type 510) against the cost centers. The faculty library and the branch library represent a special case because each of them, as a rule, is listed as an independent cost center that is not further subdivided. Here, it is to be differentiated whether the library is the sole user or merely a co-user of the building. In the first case, the cost allocation is not applicable; the value of the cost type is identical with that of the cost center. In the second case, the square meter ratio is used; that means that depreciations are assigned to the library in relation to the library's proportion of the main usable space in the co-used building. The depreciations against the moveable material assets as well as against intangible assets (cost types 520 and 530) can be assigned directly to the cost centers on the basis of the stocktaking carried out. Cost center related data about stock and useful life of assets offer important information for the coordinated planning of future replacement and expansion investments.

In LIBRARYMANAGER, the offsetting of the cost types against the cost centers runs automatically for the entire cost type groups. All that needs to be determined is the ratio values to be entered for each cost center (e.g. the square meter value of each cost center). Provided that LIBRARYMANAGER is used, the time spent making the initial cost center accounting is thus limited to about two work-weeks for a full-time employee. In the continuance phase, a further reduction of the time required can be reckoned with since the software part of the accounting model has been constructed.

The results of the cost allocation to the cost centers is represented in so-called operation sheets, which for each cost center lists the values of the cost type accounting allocated to it. In LIBRARYMANAGER, the operation sheets are differentially illustrated in the report function. *Figure 6* shows the results of the cost center accounting for University and Regional Library of Münster, whereby the library's 35 cost centers are consolidated to central service areas. The relationship of the cost centers, which directly serve the use, to the service areas that are responsible for the media processing becomes visible. The cost proportion of the overhead cost centers (administration, internal service operation, computing services) is also displayed.

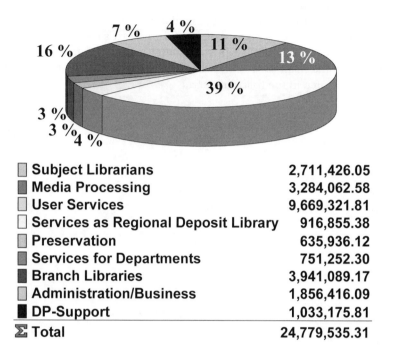

▨ **Subject Librarians**	**2,711,426.05**
▨ **Media Processing**	**3,284,062.58**
☐ **User Services**	**9,669,321.81**
☐ **Services as Regional Deposit Library**	**916,855.38**
▨ **Preservation**	**635,936.12**
▨ **Services for Departments**	**751,252.30**
▨ **Branch Libraries**	**3,941,089.17**
☐ **Administration/Business**	**1,856,416.09**
▧ **DP-Support**	**1,033,175.81**
Σ Total	**24,779,535.31**

Fig. 6: Cost of the Service Areas - University and Regional Library of Münster

   In contrast to many private-sector companies, in which cost controlling plays an essential role, cost controlling has a rather limited significance in university libraries. The department and unit heads can, as a rule, scarcely influence the cost level and cost development in their service areas. At the most, exclusively the running administrative costs, which altogether represent only a marginal amount, are their responsibility and are thereby steerable on the cost center level. Decisions about providing the cost centers with resources, especially in regards to the staff capacity and assets, are made by the library's management, often including the heads of the university. A cost controlling on the unit and departmental level, let us say in the form of analysis of the cost divergence, seems only meaningful when this organizational level has autonomously managed budgets at their disposal. Examples for libraries that practice an internal budgeting of units or departments are at present scarcely found and they are all municipal libraries (cf. Kranstedt/Wiemers 1997, 55ff.; Ceynowa 1994, chap. II).

In the context of the process oriented accounting model, the cost center accounting is primarily used to allocate of the li-brary's costs to different processes. The allocation is first done to the sub-processes related to cost centers and then to the main processes overlapping cost centers. This sequence of steps is presented in the following part.

4   Activity based costing

4.1   Building Hypotheses about the Main Processes

For the production of the services offered by the library, a multitude of processes are necessary. Those, as a rule, extend across several departments or cost centers. Activity based costing aims at the illustration of the cost emergence for all steps of the production process up to the finished service product. For this purpose, the partial services that are rendered within the cost centers are analyzed and evaluated in regards to the resources required by them. These partial services are then brought together in a cost center overlapping way to build main processes, which represent the services and thereby the cost units of the library. The library products are thus to be understood as department overlapping process sequences that arise by linking partial services together. Due to its procedural structure, every library product can conversely be divided up into its constituent sub-processes. The activity based costing thereby creates the possibility of differentially comprehending the resource consumption and the costs of a service along the path of its production. Optimizing strategies that aim at an improvement of the cost situation can therefore intervene directly into the process structure of the library products.

The theoretical and methodical bases of the activity based costing have been explained in chapter 1.4. In the following, the procedural steps of the practical implementation of this accounting systems into the library is described. The assessment of the sub-processes and their cost-center-overlapping connection to the main processes lie at the center of the modeling of the library's process structure. Identifying the main process profile, on the one hand, and working out the sub-process structure, on the other hand, should hereby be done in the mixed top-down planning: Provisional assumptions about the central main processes of the library guide the sub-process analysis on the cost center level. The results of the latter analysis in turn can lead to a new formulation of the outline of the main processes. In this way, the main process analysis and sub-process analysis support each other in an iterative procedure that step by step leads to a complete differentiation of the process structure of the library (cf. Mayer 1996, 52; Kaufmann 1997, 216f.). The answer to the question: „Which and how many main processes are to be differentiated?" totally depends on the purpose of use of the cost data to be ascertained. The main process structure is thus derived from: the primary cost accounting goals, the internal and external information needs, the essential decision situations, and the special features of the task profile. The production of the main process scheme is in essence the task of the library's governing body. In the project libraries, the following main process catalog was developed. It is divided up into ten groups:

Main process group 1: collection building
(acquiring, cataloging, binding, technical processing)

- textbooks
- monographs
- periodicals
- digital information carriers
- other non-book materials

Main process group 2: information services

- reference service
- subject information
- online enquiries (information mediation site)
- internet based information services (e.g. access to networked CD-ROM data banks, OPAC)
- supporting in-house use

Main process group 3: loans

- loaning open-shelf book stock
- loaning provided media (out of closed stacks)

Main process group 4: inter-library loans

- delivering monographs/periodical articles (conventional inter-library lending)
- ordering and providing monographs/periodical articles (conventional inter-library borrowing)
- electronic document delivery

Main process group 5: user courses

- library instruction for users
- user instruction courses for databases and enquiry instruments

Main process group 6: archive and restoration services

- producing microfilms and microfiche

- digitalizing
- Conservation
- restoration
- mass deacidifying measures

Main process group 7: providing historical/ endangered material (processing, use, references)

Main process group 8: exhibition and events

Main process group 9: special services, e.g.:
- DFG special subject field
- regional library tasks
- services for faculty-/institute libraries

Main process group 10: internal services
- library management and administration
- computing service
- public relations work

This structure of the central main processes of the library offers an adequate orientational framework for the structuring of the sub-processes on the cost center level. Due to its primarily heuristic function, the main process catalog should just be used as a guideline for dividing up the service structure within the units and departments. The main process catalog is designed primarily from the perspective of the service recipient, i.e. the user. This is evident for the main process groups 2 to 5, as well as 7 and 8. In regards to groups 1 and 6, an objection can be raised that it is here merely the matter of preliminary work. It which is not directly taken over from the user and thus should not be listed as an independent main process. However, given the phase model of service, that judgment is untenable. The acquisition, cataloging, and relegation of information resources represent structural processes and are thus just as much integral components of library service as execution processes like lending and inter-library lending (main process groups 3 and 4).

The complete service catalog of the library only arises out of the interplay between structural processes (potential phase of service performances) and execution processes (the process phase). This is pointed up by the process hierarchy in chapter 1.4. For instance, main processes such as „collection building", „loans", and „inter-library loans" could be consolidated into the business process „providing media for use". On the other hand, process connections are feasible that exclusively bring main execution processes together to form higher-level service modules. One option is linking process groups 2 to 5 together to make the business process „rendering user services". Such higher-level service areas can then, for their part, again be segmented from viewpoints that are, so to speak, „vertical" in regards to the principles of sub-division of the main process catalog. For instance, the following sub-process-es can be brought together to form the service product „providing textbooks":

- „acquiring textbooks", „cataloging textbooks", etc., (main process group 1)

- „loaning text-books", „reshelving textbooks", etc. (main process group 3)

- „managing student assistants for the textbook collection" (main process group 10)

These examples show that it depends exclusively on the given information need, or as the case may be, the cost accounting objective, as to how the sub-processes are linked together to form a higher-level process structure. The main process- or product catalog of the library thus represents only one of many possibilities derived from the data pool of sub-processes. This becomes clear when looking at the product group 9 „special services". The calculation of special tasks, project service, etc. listed in this group requires, as a rule, combining the partial services from the rest of the main process groups. Thus for instance, the regional library task dealing with legal deposit media is made up of sub-processes like „searching for and ordering legal deposit media", „subject indexing legal deposit media", „providing legal deposit media for in-house use", „microfilming legal deposit periodicals", etc. As can be seen, this task is made up of activities running through the main processes 1 to 6. The product group 9 thus describes - analogous to the example given above - ser-vice structures that are vertical in regards to the rest of the main processes. Consequently the calculation requires „ripping" partial segments „out" of those processes.

Finally, the product group 10 „internal services" puts together those ad-ministrative processes that support the core business of the library without di-rectly adding value themselves. Since these process do not have any direct use for the library user, the cost arising here should especially be examined criti-cally as to what justifies their being shown as a independent process group.

4.2 Sub-Process analysis on the Cost Center Level

The identification and delimitation of the sub-processes represent the decisive step of the process modeling. The sub-processes are evaluated in regards to capacity requirement and occurrence of cost. They make up the basic elements of data storage for the activity based costing and evaluation is done by selecting and combining the sub-processes. Thus the structure of the cost centers has to be sufficiently precise and subdivided in order to enable manifold and differentiated information- and management analyses. In contrast to the structuring of the main process, the task analysis should be done bottom-up: In an interview with the section heads directly responsible for the operating business, the work steps of the department are to be identified and delimited. A rough structuring of the task volume of their work area by the section heads before-hand could serve as a guideline for the activity analysis. A top-down procedure, i.e. producing the sub-process lists only by talking with the heads of the department and of the unit, is not recommended for this step of the process modeling. The experience of the project libraries shows, that those responsible, as a rule, do not have the necessary detailed knowledge of the working sequences of their organizational units. It is just as inadequate to base the assessment of the sub-processes exclusively on the analysis of the available activity- and site description as well as on the existing work- and organizational plan. These are oftentimes too general or to antiquated.

The basis of the sub-process delimitation should always be the main process catalog defined beforehand. In interviews with the responsible section heads, the difference of formally identical work steps (e.g. cataloging) for different main processes, needs to be inquired about. For instance, the sub-process „cataloging legal deposit media" is to be listed separately. Due to a high proportion of gray literature, external data can only be limitedly used and correspondingly, a clearly higher accession effort has to be reckoned with, as in the case of acquired media. If, on the other hand, no difference between the regular course of business and the processing of special tasks is distinguishable for the employees, further differentiation of the sub-process is pointless. Thus, for instance, it does not make a difference for the sub-processes of loans whether purchased monographs or legal deposit pieces are recorded. The proportion of costs and capacity to be assigned to the circulation of legal deposit media can be illustrated on the basis of the output ratio between the legal deposit media and the purchase media issued. It can then be assigned correspondingly to the main process level. Around 5% of the annual loans at University and Regional Library of Münster are related to legal deposit media. Correspondingly, 5% of the costs and capacities of the sub-processes „recording loans", „recording returns", etc. in the cost center „local loans" are to be assigned to the main process „providing legal deposit media".

As was already emphasized in chapter 1.4, there is no procedural rule in the sense of a uniform construction instruction for the identification and de-limitation of sub-processes. The question, as to which and how many sub-processes are to be differentiated, depends exclusively on the library's con-crete cost accounting- and management objectives. The analysis of the sub-processes thereby depends on the given individual needs, and does not fit into a ridged scheme. The project library experienced, however, that interviewing the section heads relatively quickly leads a „stable" process structure. The structure does usually not exceed the magnitude of approximately 10 to 15 sub-processes per cost center. The sub-process list from University and Re-gional Library of Münster is exemplarily printed in the appendix. It is ordered by the library's cost centers. Only the branch libraries, whose process struc-tures in essence represent an extract out of the process profile of the central library, have been removed. This list has already proved itself in several sub-sequent undertakings to be a useful framework of orientation. It can be used by other libraries to attain a quick construction of a process structure adapted to their own service profile by streamlining or augmenting correspondingly.

Two problems in the practice of sub-process assessment occurred again and again. On the one hand, an extremely high degree of itemization of the processes is often strived for, which results in an overly complex and obscure process structure. For instance, the project libraries dealt with a government agency that differentiated 600 sub-processes for their 10 employees. The dis-section of a cost center's task spectrum should end where the one uninterrupt-ed work step leads to a performance element. The activities „checking the order data", „selecting the supplier" and „sending the order", for instance, should be combined to one sub-process „ordering media".

On the other hand, vagueness occasionally arises in regards to where one process begins and where it ends. This question primarily occurs when assess-ing the working time carried out. It expresses itself as uncertainty about whether a certain work step is to be assigned to the respective upstream or downstream sub-process. Therefore, it can be helpful to describe the starting event, and the concluding event, of a process. For the sub-process „scanning the document" the starting event is defined as „document is available for scanning" and the concluding event as „document exists as a file". The con-cluding event of a given foregoing sub-process represents, as a rule, the start-ing event of a given subsequent process.

The sequence of process and event partially described here leads to the concept of the so-called activity chain steered by event, when it is applied to all steps of the service performance,. It is often used in the economic modeling of working processes (cf. Scheer 1997, 50ff.; Staud 1999, 45ff.). According to this concept, the course of business shows a complex function interdependence in which events trigger processes and processes result in events. Graphic notations allowing for software supported modeling of course of business have been developed for this process oriented description of the company's processes and events. Thus, for instance, in the modeling tool ARIS, events are illustrated by hexagons, and processes by rounded squares. Both can be chained together to arbitrary complex flow diagrams by means of logical operators or their graphic symbols (cf. Scheer 1998, 18ff.; Finkeißen 1997 and Kaeseler 1996 give an overview of the tools presently offered for activity analysis). Using such process modeler allows a detailed documentation of the business processes. It causes, however, a high execution effort, so that its application is hardly possible. This hold, at least, in the implementation phase of the process accounting The exact delimitation of the processes by the assignment of triggering and concluding events, nevertheless represents an important means of help for the construction of the sub-process structure of the cost centers.

Furthermore, in the framework of definition and delimitation of the sub-processes, the differentiation between two fundamentally different process types is important: processes depending on the activity quantity and processes independent of the activity quantity. Sub-processes depending on the activity quantity (daq) vary in the number of their executions depending on the volume of services to be rendered in the cost center. In other words, for daq-processes, the necessary time spent and correspondingly the costs to be assigned are directly dependent on the produced amount of services. This amount is expressed by the cost driver of the process. For instance, the staff consumption required for the execution of the process „accessioning media" depends directly upon the number of acquired media: If a accessioning process requires four minutes, 467 manhours are to be rated for 7,000 acquired media, and for 5,000 media, is only 333 manhours. The capacity consumption of daq-processes amounts proportionally to the rendered volume of services (cf. Mayer 1998, 13).

On the other hand, sub-processes independent of the activity quantity (iaq) are independent of the volume of services rendered in a cost center. They occur by the mere existence of the cost center and serve in preparation and support of the daq-processes. Examples for iaq-processes are „heading the

department", „tending to the project execution", etc. The differentiation between these process types is primarily relevant for the calculation of the costs,
which is described in chapter 4.4. For calculating the costs of a process, the
costs caused by the iaq-sub-processes are allocated to the daq-sub-processes
in proportion to the capacity consumption of those daq-sub-processes.

Subsequent to the identification of the sub-processes, the amount of staff
capacity consumed by every sub-process is to be determined. According to
the percentage proportion that the sub-process has of the total employee capacity available to the cost center, the cost center costs are then distributed to
the sub-processes. Since the sub-processes' capacity consumption makes up
the basis of their cost debiting, the ascertainment of the working time to be
expended per sub-process obtains a key function in activity based costing.

4.3   Assessment of the Working Time

The proportion of time the sub-processes have of the total working time
available to the cost center can either be ascertained on the basis of time logging or by estimation. If the estimation procedure is used, every employee in
the cost center has to distribute his whole work capacity in percentage terms
to the sub-processes carried out by him. According to the given percentage
values, the employee's annual manhours are then offset against the sub-processes. For a full-time employee, the annual manhours correspond to the value of an employee year, in other words, to the annual net working time.
According to the calculation undertaken in chapter 3.2, that amounts to 1,476
working hours. For instance, if a full-time employee expends 30% of his
working time for sub-process A, 55% for sub-process B, and 15% for sub-
process C, then sub-process A is to be assigned 443 hours, sub-process B 812,
and sub-process C 221. The hours ascertained per sub-process for all of the
employees in the cost center are added. From that value, the proportion that
every sub-process has of the total staff capacity of the cost center, can be obtained. If, for instance, besides the full-time employee, a half-day worker and
a 75% employed employee also work in the cost center being considered, then
the total capacity of the cost center adds up to 3,321 hours or 2,25 employee
years. If the half-day worker is engaged in sub-process A for 130 hours per
year and the three-quarter worker for 245 hours, a total of 818 employee
hours fall upon this process. This corresponds to 25% of its total capacity of
the cost center. The proportion of time for the sub-processes B and C are to
be calculated accordingly. Thereby, the staff capacity used for every sub-pro-

cess of the cost center can be obtained as a percentage of the total capacity of the cost center.

In numerous projects for activity based costing, the time estimate is considered to be an acceptable procedure (cf. e.g. Rendenbach 1997, 237; Remer 1997, 95ff.). However, since the ascertained data are exclusively based on subjective estimations of those carrying out the process, they can hardly be verified and, correspondingly, are to be called into question. If the timeframe for the implementation of the activity based costing is not all too limited, the alternative of time logging should thus be preferred. In any case, this procedure should be employed in cost centers that have a differentiated sub-process structure. Here, experience teaches, a realistic estimation of time proportions is only possible very limitedly.

Ascertaining the process times directly includes all employees of the library, regardless of whether the procedure of time estimation, of time logging, or of a mixture of both methods has been chosen. At this point, all of the involved should be informed in detail about the construction and objectives of the cost accounting. This preferably takes place in a personnel assembly, in which those responsible for the project briefly

- explain the concept of activity based costing,

- describe the method and procedure of assessing the time, and

- present the timetable planned for the ascertainment.

It is to be emphasized that the primary purpose of ascertaining the working time consists of obtaining a measuring unit for the allocation of the cost center costs to the sub-processes. In other words, it is a matter of support for a certain offsetting step in cost accounting and not a personal performance control. The project libraries experienced a quick disappear of reservations and fears when the purpose for the time ascertainment had been made transparent and understandable for the employees. The motivation for a proper execution of the measures clearly rose. In this context, feedback of the results should also be assured. Furthermore, the approval of the staff representative for the time assessment should be obtained in any case. Practical experience shows that the preservation of the personal data anonymity represents in particular an essential concern of the staff representative. Here, an explicit agreement should be made with the staff representative, especially when the procedure of time logging is chosen. It should contain the following points:

- Time logging undertaken either manually or with the aid of an electronic assessment form will be carried out, as a general rule, autonomously and without external controls.

- The evaluation of the collected data will be undertaken exclusively by the commissioned ones responsible for the project.

- An archiving of the personal data will not be done. The time assessment sheets kept manually will be destroyed after their evaluation. In the case of ascertainment forms kept electronically, the recorded data are to be deleted.

- The data evaluation leads to process times, not to employee times. The time quantity, and not the time contribution of individual employees to this process is ascertained. The evaluation thus makes the time contribution of the employees involved in the process anonymous. Only anonymous process times may be made public and be employed in the framework of performance comparisons.

The last point of the agreement should be explained more explicitly. Experience teaches that staff representatives attach much importance on it. The time assessment at first leads to time contributions for each employee, regardless of whether it is carried out as an estimate or logging. On the basis of the ascertainment records, it is calculated, for instance, that subject librarian A expends 350 hours a year for the sub-process „subject indexing", subject librarian B uses 500 hours, and subject librarian C makes do with 200 hours. Using this time data, the performance efficiency of every subject librarian could now easily be evaluated. Given, that subject librarian A performs a subject indexing of 1,200 media, B 1,400, and C 900, then that results in a processing time of 17.5 minutes per title for subject librarian A, of 21.4 minutes for subject librarian B, and of 13.3 minutes for subject librarian C. Provided that the quality of the subject indexing is the same, subject librarian C thus works clearly quicker and thereby more efficiently than A and B. Especially the value for subject librarian B seems to point to a pronounced tendency toward work laxity. However, in the context of activity based costing, that kind of personal performance data does not matter. Corresponding to the procedure described above, only the total staff capacity employed for the sub-process „subject indexing" in the cost center *subject librarians* is of interest. It is attained by the summation of the personal values of all of the employees: It is the process time of 1,050 hours that specifies the sub-process's proportion of the cost center's total capacity, and that is needed for the further course of calculation.

Taking the quotient of process time and the total process quantity (3,500 units), results in 18 minutes as the average processing time for subject indexing. This value makes the individual time anonymous.

Choosing the time logging method, first of all the logging period is to be specified. In the project, a logging period of 10 to a maximum of 20 workdays has proven itself to be fully adequate in order to obtain representative data for those cost centers in which a continual and homogeneous workload is given. In the operative business of libraries (acquisition, provision, use) standardized, administration-like routines are dominant. Therefore, only a few cost centers are left in which the suggested logging period does not lead to valid results. Those are, for the most part, the DP-department, the general library administration, as well as the labor content to be shown for special tasks in the cost center *subject librarians*. The sub-processes of these service areas are a matter of

- irregularly occurring activities (e.g. „installing hardware", „managing student assistants"),

- activities that cannot be standardized (e.g. „planning space utilization", „taking care of trainees"), as well as

- project oriented works (e.g. „developing DP-applications", „coordinating library systems").

The time requirement of these also cannot be ascertained with adequate exactness by a significant expansion of the logging period. Thus in these cost centers, a qualified estimate of the annual proportion of time for the sub-processes should be undertaken. A time logging can obviously also be done without when the workload of a cost center is completely structured by work plans. This could be the case in local loans, the bookbinding unit, or in parts of technical services.

For all of the cost centers participating in the time logging, the chosen test period should characterized by a regular workload corresponding to the normal day-to-day business. Periods of seasonally caused peak workloads („the beginning of the semester" in the user area or „the termination of a budget year" in the acquisitions department) should be avoided. Also, times of low demand for services, let us say during the main vacation period, are to be avoided. Those temporary deviations in the workload often lead to an untypical capacity usage by individual sub-processes of the affected cost center. For instance, employees who otherwise are primarily employed with technical book processing are called up to the service counter for a short time.

Cost Center: 33 Textbook Collection						
Name: Konrad Feldt						
Working Hours per Week: 38.5 hours						
Logging Period: 09/06/1999 - 09/10/1999						

Task		Working Time in Minutes					Total
No.	Description	Mon	Tue	Wed	Thu	Fri	
1	Placing Orders	118	60	45	40	21	284
2	Accessioning Media	71	43	38	40	0	192
3	Cataloging	55	67	160	47	0	329
4	Processing Book Binder Parcels	21	25	0	48	0	94
5	Processing Media Technically	64	55	0	0	20	139
6	Executing the Final Control	20	0	45	40	5	110
7	Booking Loans	0	70	67	0	120	257
8	Booking Returns	35	79	40	120	30	304
9	Reshelving Media	48	40	60	55	15	218
10	Weeding and Selling Discarded Media	0	0	0	0	0	0
11	Managing Service Counter	26	23	15	40	15	119
12	Clearing Center User	12	0	10	30	0	52
13	Administration and Organization	10	18	0	20	14	62
	Total	480	480	480	480	240	2160

Fig. 7: Time Assessment Sheet

The following procedure is advisable for the execution of time logging: Every employee involved keeps an informal work dairy. This contains the proportions of time spent per sub-process in the course of the day. The dairy is made up of a simple notebook, in which the employee lists the sub-processes carried out by him during the workday and assigns the segments of time performed to these processes. Example: „sub-process placing orders: 8:45 - 9:30, 12:20 - 1:00, 3:12 - 3:45; sub-process accession: 10:15 - 10:45, 2:30 - 3:11; and so on". The entries of the work dairy are added up daily and are transferred to the time assessment sheet shown in *figure 7*. Since the time assessment sheet is exclusively evaluated by the project commissioner responsible, the names can be written on the ascertainment sheets. This allows direct consultation in case of evident inconsistencies and assessment mistakes. As an al-

No.	Sub-process Description	Measuring Unit Type	Volume	Staff Capacity %	Hours	EY	Costs daq	iaq	Total	Expense Ratios daq	Total
1	Placing Orders	daq media acquired - textbook material	1.726	5,90	610	0,41	23.453,27	1.291,69	24.744,96	13,59	14,34
2	Accessioning Media	daq volumes acquired - textbook material	8.251	7,59	785	0,53	30.171,24	1.661,68	31.832,92	3,66	3,86
3	Cataloging (incl. shelf register)	daq media acquired - textbook material	1.726	8,30	859	0,58	32.993,58	1.817,12	34.810,70	19,12	20,17
4	Processing Book Binder Parcels	daq parcels processed	26	1,23	127	0,09	4.889,41	269,28	5.158,69	188,05	198,41
5	Processing Media Technically	daq volumes acquired - textbook material	8.251	8,43	872	0,59	33.510,35	1.845,58	35.355,93	4,06	4,29
6	Executing the Final Control	daq volumes acquired - textbook material	8.251	2,62	271	0,18	10.414,84	573,60	10.988,44	1,26	1,33
7	Booking Loans	daq textbook material issued	261.501	20,66	2.137	1,45	82.126,18	4.523,09	86.649,27	0,31	0,33
8	Booking Returns	daq textbook material issued	261.501	20,66	2.137	1,45	82.126,18	4.523,09	86.649,27	0,31	0,33
9	Reshelving Media	daq textbook material issued	261.501	13,43	1.389	0,94	53.386,00	2.940,23	56.326,23	0,20	0,22
10	Weeding and Selling Discarded Media	daq textbook material sold	8.573	5,96	617	0,42	23.691,77	1.304,82	24.996,59	2,76	2,92
11	Managing Service Counter	iaq		1,88	195	0,13		7.473,24			
12	Clearing Center User Services	iaq		1,91	198	0,13		7.592,50			
13	Administration and Organization	iaq		1,43	148	0,10		5.684,44			
	Total			100,00	10.345	7,00	376.762,82	20.750,18	397.513,00		

Fig. 8: The Assignment of Capacity and of Cost to the Sub-Process Level Using the Example of the Textbook Collection.

ternative to manual time logging, as it is exemplarily represented in *figure 7*, the electronic form of the time assessment module in LIBRARYMANAGER can be used. The preservation of the data anonymity is here ensured by the entry of employee- and supervisor passwords.

After the employees have time-logged for the number of workdays agreed upon, the assessment sheets go back to the project commissioner. In a first step, the values of all of the logging days are added together per employee for every sub-process. In a second step, the values of all of the sub-processes are summed up to a total logging time. The employee exclusively writes the process related working times down, but does not write down breaks and allowances. Therefore, the total logging time corresponds with the net working time of the employee during the assessment period. Given the total logging time the percentage proportion of every process can then be ascertained. From this step on, the further calculation procedure runs analogous to the procedure describe above in the case of time estimation. This means, the annual manhours of the employee are distributed to the sub-processes according to the ascertained percentage proportion, and so on.

In LIBRARYMANAGER, the calculation steps described are automatically carried out. Additionally, the capacity proportions calculated are transferred directly from the time assessment module to the cost accounting module. Since the manual keeping and evaluation of the ascertainment sheets involve a calculation effort that is not to be underestimated, the time logging should preferably be carried out by LIBRARYMANAGER. For the project libraries, the employees involved did not have any trouble keeping a work dairy, nor dealing with the time assessment sheets. Only occasional problems with the assignment of individual activities to the sub-processes were noticed. Thus, as long as questions and misgivings that normally arise in the forefront of the measures are clarified, the time assessment will usually be carried out smoothly within the designated test period

4.4   Assessment of the Costs

As a result of the assessment of the working time, the time proportions that the sub-processes of every cost center have of the total working time available to that cost center are obtained. *Figure 8* exemplarily shows this for the cost center textbook collection. The staff capacity employed per sub-process is shown in percentage terms, in annual hours, and in employee years (EY). For instance, the result for the sub-process „placing orders" is a proportion of 5.90% of the cost center's total staff capacity. This corresponds to 610 annual hours, or 0,41 employee years. The costs of the cost centers are then distributed to the sub-processes proportional to the proportion of capacity that each sub-process has of the total staff capacity of the cost center. This leads to the costs of the sub-processes for an accounting period being considered. The process „placing orders" is thus burdened with 5.9% of the cost center's total costs of 397,513 DM, and accordingly gets 23,453 DM assigned to it. All of the other sub-processes of the cost center are done similarly. Thus, the sum of the sub-process costs corresponds to the total costs of the cost center.

This clearing system is characterized by allocating all existing costs proportional to the staff capacity used for a process. Therefore, not only the staff costs are distributed this way, but also the costs for all consumed resources (space, outfitting, office material, etc.) (cf. Mayer 1998, 13ff.). As was shown in chapter 1.4, this procedure is reasonable, since the costs occurring in service companies are substantially determined by the number of employees (e.g. in regards to the space, office furniture, DP-outfitting). Hence, the costs can be distributed to the sub-processes in relation to the staff capacity used by each given sub-process (cf. Niemand 1996, 100). LIBRARYMANAGER allows the printout of reports that lists the sub-processes divided according to resource types - staff costs, administrative costs, operating costs, depreciations. It thus allows a differentiated view of the cost structures on the sub-process level.

Particularly for output costing and consolidated cost ratios for external information needs, it could be necessary to offset the costs of a cost center which are independent of the activity quantity against that cost center's sub-processes depending on the activity quantity. The example of *figure 8* deals with the costs of the iaq-processes „managing service counter", „clearing center user services" and „administration and organization". Those together constitute 20,750 DM and take up a staff capacity of 0.36 employee years (541 hours). The cost allocation is done by offsetting the total costs of the iaq-sub-processes against the daq-sub-processes according to the capacity consumption of those daq-sub-processes. For this purpose, the quotient of the sum of the iaq-costs (20,750 DM) and the total staff capacity of the daq-sub-processes (in the example 6.64 EY) is calculated. The result represents the costs that are to be assigned to an daq employee year (3,125 DM). This value is then multiplied with the staff capacity proportion of every daq-sub-process in the cost center, and results in the iaq-costs to be assigned to each given daq-sub-process. For instance, 4,523 DM (1.45 EY x 3,125 DM) of iaq-costs are to be assigned to the sub-process „booking loans" of the textbook collection, since it uses up 1.45 employee years. Adding the daq-costs (82,126 DM) and the iaq-costs of the sub-processes results in its total costs of 86,649 DM.

The core idea of activity based costing is the provision of a flexible data pool that is suitable for manifold evaluation calculations. Therefore, the daq-costs and the iaq-costs are shown in LIBRARYMANAGER both separate, as well as consolidated to total costs. Thus, the relevant data are at hand for each given decision-making situation. The relationship of daq-processes to iaq-processes constitutes an interesting ratio. It informs about the proportion of capacity and costs for processes not directly related to the output. The ratio can be examined in intercompany performance comparisons. Usually, a high portion of processes neutral to the amount of performance in a cost center indicates inadequate work structuring and organizational design. In addition, the analysis of iaq-processes shows that the library's overhead costs are generally rated too low, when just regarding pertinent cost centers like *general administration, computing services,* and *technical services*. A realistic picture does not arise until the services of administration, leadership, and coordination within the department are also included. They can for their part be examined in regards to their necessity in comparison to other libraries. At the University and Regional Library of Münster, for instance, the iaq-processes of all of the cost centers use up a total of 7 employee years, in other words, 10,332 annual hours.

4.5 Identifying the Cost Driver

In the next step, measuring units for determining the process activity are ascertained for all sub-processes depending on the activity quantity. These so-called cost drivers serve, as was explained in chapter 1.4, the assessment of the process quantity produced by a sub-process. For choosing the measuring units, the definition of the service object needs to be very exact and tailored for each considered process. For instance, the number of student assistant rather than the total weekly hours of student assistants is to be applied as cost driver for the process „managing student assistants". The process activities, like completion of an employment contract, maintaining a vacation file, etc., occur in each given case „per head". The following cost drivers were defined for the sub-processes mentioned in the example in *figure 8*:

- The number of media acquired for the processes „placing orders" and „cataloging";

- the number of volumes acquired for the processes „accession", „processing textbook material technically", „executing the final control";

- the number of media issued for the processes „booking loans", „booking returns", and „reshelving media";

- the number of parcels processed for the process „processing book binder parcels";

- the number of textbook material sold for the process „weeding and selling discarded media".

The service volume to be assigned to a given measuring unit can usually be taken from the statistics kept within the cost center. In the example the volume is illustrated in the column „volume of measuring unit". For those sub-processes, for which no figures exist for the process quantity, an estimated value should be worked with in the implementation phase of the cost accounting. The estimates can be validated in the continuation phase, for instance, by random sample analyses.

As was described in chapter 1.4, the cost driver is the measuring unit for the consumption of resources used by processes. The number of cost driver units to be assigned to a process determines the number of required executions of the process. In turn, it thereby also determines the resources and costs needed for the process. The cost driver thus represents the central cost determinant of the processes. This dependency, however, may not be interpreted to the effect that the costs rise by a unit cost rate of a service unit for every additional execution of the process. This direct correlation of process quantity and level of cost is, as a rule, valid exclusively for the marginal portion that variable costs make up of the costs. For instance, the costs for shipping materials and postage sink proportional to the decrease in the number of interlibrary loan orders delivered conventionally.

However, for the dominant fixed-cost portion of the costs (in particular the staff costs) a direct dependency on the cost driver quantity does not exit. Fixed costs cannot be influenced by changes in the activity quantity within each of their commitment periods. Thus, for constant costs, the reduction of process quantity inevitably leads to a rise of costs to be shown per activity unit. For instance, if the lending of the textbook collection (in the example, 261.501 loans) sinks by 40,000, the costs of the sub-processes „booking loans", „booking returns", and „reshelving media" (daq) remain unchanged. Those are fixed costs for staff, space, and outfitting. The minimal commitment period is given by the six month period of the contracts for the student assistants. On the other hand, the expense ratio for a textbook loan will rise. The costs are no longer to be divided by the process quantity of 261,501 issued media units, but rather by that value reduced by 40,000 units. A change in the cost driver quantity demonstrates only a need for capacity adjustment, which has to be actualized by management decisions. Possible reactions are a shifting of staff, or the termination of student assistant contracts (cf. Niemand 1996, 98f.).

For effective interventions, the determination of the cost driver quantity on the basis of the actual value of one accounting period, however, does not suffice. For cost oriented capacity planning, it is not decisive how many processes are actually performed within a period. It rather matters, how many processes could be performed on the basis of the given resources and corresponding costs. Thus, normalized values are needed that describe the cost driver quantity producible under regular work conditions. The achievement potential accomplishable under normal conditions describes the amount of available process executions. The activity volume rendered de facto during a period describes the amount of needed process executions. Only the juxtaposition of the available process executions to the actually used ones, i.e., of the provided resources to the used resources, allows the proportion of used-capacity and of idle-capacity costs to be shown. This proportion enables precise intervention into the built up achievement potential (cf. Cooper/Kaplan 1995, 49f.). Lets say, in the textbook collection the provided resources lead to a normal capacity of 300,000 loans. Then, a used-capacity of 87% (261,501 / 300,000 x 100) can be calculated on the basis of the actual value of the example. Accordingly, 13% of the costs of the processes involved represent the idle-capacity costs, in other words, the costs of process executions available, but not needed. The exemplarily assumed decrease of loans by 40,000 units would cause the idle-capacity cost proportion of the processes to rise to 26%.

The determination of the cost driver quantity on the basis of normalized values requires thought about the economical performance rate of library processes. This requires, at least in the implementation phase of the cost accounting, an analysis effort that is too high. Hence, the available actual data of the accounting period considered should be used to begin with. The ascertainment of the cost driver quantity possible considering the given resources should then take place in the course of the cost oriented capacity planning and -steering. This procedure will be described in chapter 5.2. The quantities of the textbook collection shown in *figure 8* represent the actual value of the reference period 1997. By definition, process quantities cannot be ascertained for the sub-processes independent of the activity quantity.

4.6 Calculation of the Process Cost Rates and Processing Times

The calculation of the process cost rate is done by simple division of the costs of a sub-process by the cost driver quantity assigned to it. In the calculation shown in *figure 8*, 30,171 DM of daq-process costs and a process activity of 8,251 processed media units has been ascertained for the sub-process „accessioning textbook material". The quotient of the costs divided by the process quantity thus results in a process cost rate of 3.66 DM. This value represents the average costs of accessioning one media unit. Regarding the total costs of a sub-process, i.e., including the according iaq-cost proportion, the process cost rate will raise to 3.86 DM. Correspondingly, the quotient of the employee capacity taken up by the process divided by the process quantity results in the processing time. This is the average time requirement for a single execution of the sub-process. In the example this is 5.7 minutes per accession operation.

It should be kept in mind, that the calculated process cost rates do not take different employment relationships and salary scales into account. If the sub-process „accession", for instance, were carried out exclusively by the section head of the textbook collection, then this process would be undervalued in terms of costs by the offsetting procedure shown (cf. Remer 1977, 122). That, however, does not constitute an objection against the accounting approach since the latter aims exclusively at the determination of sub-process costs and sub-process cost rates occurring on the average in regards to the cost center's total costs. The described problem arose in the practice of the project libraries only in a few exceptional cases. Moreover, it is always possible to withhold certain cost elements of a cost center out of the described calculation steps. They can be assigned directly to a certain sub-process. This option, which is, however, only rarely used in the practice of activity based costing (cf. Rendenbach 1997, 237f.; Mayer 1998, 15), is also supported by LIBRARYMANAGER.

4.7 Linking the Sub-Processes together to form Main Processes

The ascertainment of the process cost rates and of the processing times conclude the construction of the process model. As was explained in chapter 1.4, the following rates now exist for every library sub-process depending on the activity quantity:

- The staff capacity of the sub-process, for instance, 0.59 employee years (872 annual hours) for the process „processing media technically" in the cost center *textbook collection.*

- The costs of the sub-process, which are shown as pure daq-costs as well as the costs including the offset iaq-cost proportion. For the process „processing media technically", daq-process costs of 33,510 DM and total costs of 35,356 DM are shown for the reference year 1997.

- The cost driver quantity of the sub-process during the accounting period.

- The process cost rate of the sub-process, in the example 4,06 DM (daq), respectively 4,29 DM (total) for the technical processing of a media unit.

- The processing time of the sub-process, 6.3 minutes for the technical processing of a media unit in the example.

Only cost and capacity proportions can be shown for the processes independent of the activity quantity since, according to their definition, cost driver quantities do not exist. The calculation of the library's main processes is done according to the procedure described in chapter 1.4 by bringing together the sub-processes belonging together due to the matter to form a main process. A sub-process can either be completely or partially assigned to a main process.

Figure 9 illustrates how sub-processes are connected together to make main processes. The example of acquiring and processing legal deposit media (monographs) at University and Regional Library of Münster is used. The processes of searching, requesting, accessioning, and cataloging the legal deposit media arise in the cost center *integrated processing of legal deposit media.* Their entire costs are to be entered into the main process „processing legal deposit media". The process „subject indexing legal deposit media" is listed in the cost center *subject librarians* as an independent sub-process. Likewise, the sub-processes „checking subject indexing", „recording keyword chains", and „adding new keyword records", which are performed in the cost center *subject catalog,* are each shown separately for the legal deposit media and for the purchase media. The processing of legal deposit media or purchased media does not make any difference for the sub-process „processing legal deposit media technically" in the cost center *technical book processing* and „filing accessions" in the cost center *stacks.* The costs of these sub-processes can therefore be partially distributed to the main processes corresponding with the output ratio between the processed legal deposit- and purchase copies. For instance, a total of 37,234 accessions were relegated in the reference year 1997. 6,695 units or 18% or these are legal deposit copies. Correspondingly, the main process „processing legal deposit media" is to be assigned 18% of the costs of the sub-process „filing accessions", in the example 5,308 DM.

Total: 300,869 DM

Filing Accessions	5,308
Technical Processing	11,223
Adding New Keyword Records	37,903
Recording Keyword Chains	7,485
Checking Subject Indexing	4,343
Subject Indexing Legal Deposit Monographs	28,369
Cataloguing Legal Deposit Monographs	86,144
Accessioning Legal Deposit Monographs	37,645
Requestion Legal Deposit Monographs	37,876
Searching for Legal Deposit Monographs	44,573

Fig. 9: Main Process - Providing Legal Deposit Media (Monographs)

In *figure 9*, the central concern of the activity based costing, namely the interface-analysis of the services, becomes obvious once again. The main process under consideration is made up of process contributions from a total of five cost centers. It cause the total cost of 300,869 DM for the acquiring and processing of legal deposit media. For the 6,695 legal deposit copies processed in 1997, a process cost rate of 44,90 DM can be calculated. Without the activity based costing, the analysis would have inevitably had to limit itself to the costs of the cost center *integrated processing of legal deposit media*. The costs shown here amount to 206,238 DM, and lead to an expense ratio of 30,80 DM. The costs of the acquisition and processing of the legal deposit media would have thus been clearly undervalued. This is an example of how the traditional, cost-center-oriented approach lets the actual costs of service production disappear into a „black hole". The processing costs for legal deposit monographs can, in a further step, be complemented by a) the costs of acquiring and accessioning legal deposit periodicals and b) the standby costs of legal deposit media in loan circulation and in-house use. Additionally taking the costs of the main processes „processing the Bibliography of North Rhein-Westfalia" and „processing the historical collections in North-Rhine Westphalia „, results in the costs of the business process „fulfilling the regional library task". The regional library services are illustratable in the form of a process hierarchy, in which the business processes arise out of main processes linked together, which for their parts again arise out of sub-processes linked together.

The sub-processes make up the building blocks of the process hierarchy and the latter is constructed corresponding to each given accounting purpose. They have, as was shown in chapter 1.4, a key position in the concept of activity based costing. As a general rule, sub-processes are assigned two-dimensionally: on the one hand, to the cost center carrying them out, and on the other hand, completely or partially to the main processes (cf. Remer 1997, 134f.). They thereby perform the transfer of the cost center costs to main process costs, and thus make enable the analysis of the entire service flow. At the same time, the capacity related and cost related evaluation of the sub-processes generates a data storage usable for manifold cost accounting purposes. The way that sub-processes are consolidated to higher-level service structures (main processes, business processes...), depends exclusively on the chosen cost accounting- and management objectives. This will once again be elucidated exemplarily in the following by means of the provision of textbook material at University and Regional Library of Münster.

Figure 8 shows the sub-processes listed in the cost center *textbook collection* for the acquisition, processing, and loaning of textbook material. For the complete assessment of the costs connected with the provision of textbook material, the sub-process „selecting textbook material" listed in the cost center *subject librarians* is additionally to be drawn in. This sub-process takes up 0.35 employee years and causes costs of 40,398 DM. Furthermore, the process „managing student assistants" in the cost center *general administration* is to be taken into account. As the example statement of account in chapter 1.4 shows, that one takes up costs of 27,000 DM in the reference year 1997. For the 70 student assistants employed by the library this results in a process cost rate of 396 DM. Since the textbook collection employs 9 student assistants, it is, accordingly, to be allocated 3,564 DM administrative costs for student assistants. Finally, the cost proportion of the process „providing server performance for the loan system and cataloging" performed in the DP-department is to be drawn in. It is to be allocated proportionally to the number of issue desks and cataloging sites installed in the textbook collection.

For simplicity's sake, however, those cost proportions should not be further considered in the following.

The total cost of the main process „providing textbook material" are the sum of the process costs of all of the sub-processes in the cost center *textbook collection* (397,513 DM) plus the cost of the process „selecting textbook material" (40,398) and the cost proportion of the process „managing student assistants" (3,564 DM). This amounts to 441,475 DM. The linking together of the sub-processes involved, thus leads to an exact cost picture. It not only ascertains the costs directly related to the services, but also the proportionate overhead costs. If one additionally takes the operating costs and the depreciation charges of the textbook collection's user area (23,200 DM; cost center 33.2 on the chart of functional accounts), and the media budget for the textbook collection (614,000 DM), a highly aggregated cost statement will be attained: Providing students with the basic textbook material at University and Regional Library of Münster in 1997 caused costs of 1,078,200 DM and took up 4.3% of the library's total costs. That kind of cost information is primarily relevant for external decision makers. For instance, it can come into play in target agreements between the university heads and the library, or be used in the context of inter-university performance comparisons.

For the purposes of internal library steerage, the process sequences of the media provision that are primarily significant are the ones that differ significantly from the work steps of the regular course of business. Of interest are, for instance, multiple copies and a low accessibility effort. Ranked among these is the process „selecting textbook material" in the cost center *subject librarians* as well as the processes of acquisition and processing in the cost center *textbook collection* (in *figure 8*, sub-processes 1 through 6, and the sub-process 10). Since a short processing time is essential particularly for textbook material, these sub-processes are to be checked separately in regards to their efficiency. This could, for instance, be done by having their expense ratios and processing times compared with the parallel processes of the regular course of business or by inter-company benchmarking. Inasmuch as these accounting objectives are pursued, the main process „acquiring and processing textbook material" is to be shown. It merely consists of the parts of the costs of the main process „providing textbook material" that are relevant for the external information needs.

Not to be included are, to begin with, the costs of the loans of the textbook material, in other words, the sub-processes 7 thru 9 in *figure 8*. These sub-processes can for their part, be pulled together with the processes from the cost center local loans to make a general main process „lending media". This clearing channel corresponds to the main process structuring recommended in chapter 4.1. Since the student assistants of the textbook collection are primarily employed in the loan circulation, the costs of the overhead sub-process „managing student assistants" are also not to be taken into account for the main process „acquiring and processing textbook material". Just like the administrative costs of the student assistants working in the cost center „local loans", they are to be allocated to the main process „lending media". By bringing the costs of the sub-processes 1 thru 6 and 10 from the cost center *textbook collection* (167,888 DM including the offset iaq-cost proportions) together with the sub-process „selecting textbook material" (40,398 DM), a total cost of 208,286 DM can be calculated for the main process „acquiring and processing textbook material".

Another sub-process cluster results, if the relationship of the total overhead costs occurring in the library to the costs of the value added processes should be calculated. For this purpose, not only the costs of the cost centers *general administration, technical services*, etc., are to be taken into account, but also the costs of the administrative services within the departments (cf. chapter 4.4). The latter are represented by the iaq-sub-processes of the cost centers. If the costs of the all of the library's iaq-sub-processes are allocated to the main process „management and administration", the main process „providing textbook material" and its subset, the main process „acquiring and processing textbook material", are in return to be relieved of their iaq-costs proportion. In addition, the costs of the overhead process „managing student assistants" are also to be deducted from the main process „providing textbook material". The result is a reduction of the costs to be allocated to this main process amounting to a total of 24,314 DM (20,750 DM iaq-costs + 3,564 DM sub-process „managing student assistants").

The calculation examples show that it exclusively depends upon the cost accounting- and management objectives, as to how the sub-processes are linked together to form higher process sequences and how the costs and capacities are assigned accordingly. With complete differentiation of the sub-process structure in regards to capacity and costs, the applier has a multitude of combining possibilities. Each chosen main process division just one of the many cost structuring regarding the identical database. The flexibility of evaluation hereby ensures a sustainable system, that in principle can also suffice such information needs that were not foreseeable at the time of its implementation.

Moreover, in the process oriented accounting approach process elements can be brought together that are scattered over a multitude of cost centers. Thus, they can of evaluating in regards to their resource requirements. The cost transparency attained hereby is pointed out in an example: The calculation of the unit costs caused by processing conventional inter-library borrowing at University and Regional Library of Münster. The inclusion of the sub-processes listed in the cost center *inter-library loans* is rudimental ("determining routing", "sending loan forms", "processing and booking receipts", "controlling due dates", etc. Those sub-processes use up 3.9 employee years and costs of a total of 335,174 DM for the reference year. Furthermore, the costs of checking holdings for inter-library loan forms are to be determined. This service is done daily in varying time proportions by almost all staff in the upper service. It thereby represents an activity distributed over almost all of the departments of the library. Thus, it is not perceptible as an independent pool of costs when just regarding cost centers. The activity analysis, however, allows a cost analysis of this distributed activity. Moreover, the services of the cost center *reference services* supporting the checking service is to be taken into account. There support is depicted by the sub-process "supporting bibliographic services". For the sub-process "performing holding checks", a capacity requirement of a total of 7.5 employee years is calculated, for the sub-process "supporting bibliographic services" it is 2 employee years.

Together, both processes in the reference year 1997 resulted in costs of 917,440 DM, of which 888,047 DM were staff costs. The "cost hog" of the inter-library borrowing does not lie in the processes of the cost center *inter-library loans* dealing directly with the execution of the inter-library loan requests. It rather lies in the supporting checking service: 73% (!) of the total costs of 1,252,614 DM to be rated for the inter-library borrowing fall upon it. Given 45,933 successful inter-library loan requests in 1997, a process cost rate of 27.27 DM and a processing time of 26 minutes per request is calculated.

Furthermore, in activity based costing the allocation of the sub-processes of the overhead cost centers to the services produced by the library is fair according to the input involved. Thus, as was shown, the costs of the sub-process "managing student assistants" are, by using its process cost rate, offset against the main processes. In the example carried out above, a process cost rate of 396 DM was ascertained for the sub-process "managing student assistants". Accordingly, the main process "providing textbook material", was allocated the proportionate costs of 3,564 DM (9 x 396 DM), since 9 student assistants are involved in this process. In this way, 32% of the total overhead process costs occurring at University and Regional Library of Münster can be

Main Process		costs in DM	costs per unit	employee years	minutes per unit
Media Acquisition and Media Processing	textbook material	208.286	25,24	3,17	35
	monographs	2.371.065	78,09	22,57	66
	periodicals newspapers	710.446	55,54	7,97	55
	non-book materials	113.492	42,73	1,05	35
Main Process		costs in DM	costs per unit	employee years	minutes per unit
Loans	local loans	1.713.923	1,80	24,44	2
	inter-library lending	347.742	5,88	4,26	6
	inter-library borrowing	1.252.614	27,27	13,42	26
	El.Doc.Deliv. lending	17.872	6,93	0,23	8
	El.Doc.Deliv. borrowing	51.657	9,85	0,62	11
Main Process		costs in DM	costs per unit	employee years	minutes per unit
Reference Service and User Education *(Preparation and Execution)*	advising users	423.795	4,93	4,70	5
	online searches	54.910	150,03	0,51	124
	guided library tours	76.185	290,78	0,56	188
	instruct. f. CD-ROM databas.	115.283	153,30	1,08	127

Fig. 10: A selected Sample of Main Processes - University and Regional Library of Münster

directly assigned to the library services. The remaining overhead processes altogether comprise 8% of the library's total costs. For them, there is no direct connection with the operative business of the library. They describe activities like „managing material supplies", „planning space utilization", „human resource management", etc, which should be listed as the independent process group „internal services". Since these processes do not have any directly noticeable use for the library customer, the costs occurring here are to be continually examined in regards to their necessity. This could be done, for instance, by having the processes undergo a benchmarking. This process group can also be offset against the remaining main processes in relation to their employee capacity. In LIBRARYMANAGER, the option of an offsetting of the main processes proportional to the capacity is included.

As was mentioned before, the basic concerns of activity based costing are providing a data pool useable for manifold cost accounting objectives. The objection could be raised that the evaluation flexibility thus created is accompanied by the danger of uncontrollable manipulation of cost information. This objection, however, does not appear to be tenable. Indeed, the differentiation and delimitation of each process structure to be calculated is left up to the applier. Corresponding to the cost perspective chosen, the sub-processes in each given case can be combined and brought together differently to form higher-level service objects. However, 100% of the process costs are always to be distributed. So, every attempt „to calculate" a certain service „cheaply" is only done at the price of making another service expensive. The exemplary calculation of providing of textbook material clearly shows this: If the iaq-sub-processes and the proportionate costs of the process „managing student assistants" are not considered, the costs to be assigned are reduced by 24,314 DM. The costs of the main process „management and administration", however, inevitably rise by the same amount. In the same way, the applier can decide whether to consolidate the costs of lending textbook material with the costs of their purchase and processing to form a main process „providing textbook material", or whether to bring them together with the process costs of the cost center *local loans* to form the main process „lending media". Regardless of which way he chooses, the easing of the cost burden of one main process is always connected with the cost burdening of another main process. Here it is once again made clear that each main process structure chosen represents a construct, the tailoring of which is dictated exclusively by the information need of the applier. The expense and capacity rates of the sub-processes, upon which each given evaluation calculation is built, are, nevertheless, clearly fixed and cannot be manipulated.

The example shows that a degree of cost transparency is attainable that excludes manipulation possibilities. This is especially true in regards to intercompany performance comparisons. These are only informative when the process structures are identical. If, for instance, the standby times and standby costs for textbook material are to be compared, the following questions are to be clarified first: Should pure daq-costs or costs including iaq-costs be taken as a basis? Are proportionate overhead costs to be included? Should the sub-process „weeding and selling discarded media" be included or be left out of account? Only after clarifying these question the service processes to be included into the benchmarking are comparable. Then, cost differences are interpretable as efficiency differences.

Furthermore, only a cost accounting that suffices the differentiated information needs will in practice also be accepted in the long-term. A differentiated evaluation calculation inevitably requires a highly flexible calculatory instrument for the tailoring of activity based costing. In LIBRARYMAN-AGER the designing a so-called cost accounting object is possible. This leads to a still higher degree of freedom for the evaluation. From the level of the cost center accounting on, an arbitrary number of cost elements can be assigned to a cost accounting object. Above all, this option allows the inclusion of the cost centers user area, circulation area and technology and the user area of branch and faculty libraries, in the software's automated course of calculation. The *user area* and *circulation area and technology* are not offset against the sub-processes and therefore should be entered as cost accounting objects. In the chart of functional accounts they comprise the cost centers 33.2, 34.2, 34.3, 35.2, 36.2, 46, 61.2. For instance, the main process costs of the reference and loan services can be brought together with the cost center costs of the *user areas reading room, stacks, reference desk*, etc. to form a cost accounting object. The total cost of this object is then calculated automatically.

Figure 10 exemplarily shows the cost- and capacity values of University and Regional Library of Münster for the reference period 1997. The cost driver is assigned to a main process according to the service objective of a process. For instance, the number of successfully completed orders is the cost driver for the main processes of the conventional inter-library loans and of the electronic document delivery. Since the lending of teaching material is the objective of the main process „providing textbook material", the cost driver is the number of media issued. If, on the other hand, only the unit costs for acquiring and processing textbook material is calculated (cf. row 1 in *figure 10*), the cost driver could either be number of titles acquired or number of volumes acquired.

For those cases, no blanket rule for selection can be given. However, in applied activity based costing the cost driver consuming the most costs is usually chosen. Thus, in the example, for the number of acquired volumes would be the cost driver (cf. Kajüter 1997, 222; Remer 1997, 133). The expense rate of the main process represents the average costs occurring for the one-time execution of the process. This is in the same way as the process cost rate does on the sub-process level.

The time required for the construction of the activity based costing essentially depends upon whether the ascertainment of the employee capacity of the sub-processes is primarily done by time estimate or by time logging. Experience teaches, that between three and four months of a full-time employee are to need for setting up the process model of the library, if time logging using LIBRARYMANAGER is chosen. Using a time estimate for the majority of the cost centers, the time requirement is reduced by approximately a man-month. It is to be kept in mind that particularly the coordination process with the staff representative depends upon border conditions, and can scarcely be influenced by the project commissioner (meetings, duty of reporting, etc.). At the project libraries, the agreement of the staff council for the time assessment was obtained within two to six weeks. In the continuation phase, the activity based costing requires a low maintenance effort since all of the calculation routines in LIBRARYMANAGER run automatically. Subsequent assessments of the capacity requirement of sub-processes are only necessary when the operational profile of a cost center is restructured. The initial introduction of cost type accounting, cost center accounting, and activity based costing in a library takes a total of five to six employee months. Not taken into account is the time required for a) interviews by the section heads to gather information about sub-processes and b) filling time assessment sheets. The latter, however, as a rule is limited to a few work minutes per employee per day.

The performance of the constructed process model is not limited to the provision of a data pool for differentiated calculatory purposes. Beyond that, the detailed analysis of the library processes offers essential starting points for active cost management of the library services. This is especially relevant for the employee capacity taken up by the processes. A deliberate influencing of the service production factors determining the emergence and development of costs becomes possible. As was shown in chapter 1.2, costs are only symptoms of service processes consuming resources and thereby causing costs. The continual optimization of these processes as well as the demand-oriented allocation of the resources needed for their execution are thus the focal points of the management of the library costs. The fundamentals for cost management in libraries are to be explained in the following.

5   Cost Management

5.1   Strategies of Process Optimization

The most essential characteristic of the activity based costing in regards to steering aspects is the ability to build main processes across cost-centers. Whereas a sub-process is always a work step within a cost center, a main process, as a rule, unifies sub-processes from several departments. It can thus describe services that go through different organizational units. The analysis of the main processes shows how the costs of a service successively accumulate on the way through the processing stages. It becomes perceivable how an inadequate organizational and informational integration of the sub-processes involved leads to inefficiencies in service production. Like generally in the administrational area, the operational procedures in libraries are strongly oriented on individual tasks and a specialization of the employees. The calculation given in the preceding section clearly shows that. At University and Regional Library of Münster, for instance, the document delivery service involves four cost units; a total of five departments are involved in the processing of legal deposit copies.

Such fragmented processes inevitably generate a high need for coordination and organization. This is particularly true for the interface between the cost centers involved. For instance, iterated compressing and decompressing of processed media units occur while books sit, before being passed on to the next department for processing. This compels manifold routines for coordination and control. Time expenditure for preparation and distribution does not only occur once, but repetitively in every department. Furthermore, it is difficult to integrate new tasks into the traditional work structures and departmental structures. This holds especially in the area of digital information services. The acquisition and provision of electronic media, the execution of document delivery services, etc. represent relatively complex tasks. Therefore, the idea of processing them by a single agent seems reasonable, be that agent a single employee or a team. At the same time, these tasks require elements that allow an integration into already established courses of business and departmental structures. This often leads to partial insertion of the given tasks into the standard business process, while the remaining sub-processes are given to a separate functional centers. The inevitable consequence of those „carved" service operations is highly complicated process structures overloaded with variants and special cases.

Division of labor and interface-intensive service production lead to some organizational deficits. Carrying out activity based costing, the cost effects of these deficits can be made transparent and precise measures can be applied. Since the activity based costing analyzes the sub-processes running in „the backbone" of the cost centers and functional areas, measures to improve the cost situation can intervene directly into necessary process structures. At first, the sub-processes in each cost center are to undergo a critical examination, whereby the following questions in particular should be asked (cf. Niemand 1996, 91f.): Which consequences would the discontinuation of the sub-processes have? (Is the annual report of the department really needed by the management? Is the checking of keyword chains necessary?) Can processes executed sequentially also be done parallel? (Can the catalog data generated in the regular course of business simultaneously be used for regional bibliography?) Can two activities running separately be brought together to one sub-process? (Can accession and the processing of invoices be completed in one operation?) Which activities could be done without if the sub-process were to be carried out by only one employee? (Could reconciliation processes and coordination processes be avoided if all of the material purchasing where to be in the hands of one person?) What advantages does the sub-process have for the library's customers? (When a classified arrangement of books is given, is subject indexing necessary at all?) How would the process run, given an optimal DP-support? (How much staff capacity would be set free if business transactions with the book store were to be conducted electronically.) The gains of costs and of capacity by the optimization measures introduced can be calculated exactly since the sub-processes affected are evaluated in regards to employee usage and cost occurrence. These insights can be used, for instance, for the redirection of resources.

In a second step, the process contributions to the core processes of a library should be examined. By core processes, the central services like loans, document delivery, subject information, etc. are meant. The focal point here is the optimization of the production flow throughout all of the organizational units involved. The partial steps of the service production can be analyzed with regards to the procedural organization. (e.g. from the receipt of order up to processing the invoice (electronic delivery service), or from the selection of media up to the relegation (media processing)). The involved sub-processes of the cost centers are, thus, not considered as isolated, but rather as connected in the framework of their interface overlapping linkage with the main processes. From this perspective, departments and other functional centers are rather „stumbling blocks" to a smooth process execution than obvious subdivisions of the course of business. The analysis of the library's core processes can thus help to overcome the inadequacies of function-oriented work structures. The deficits of many interfaces and division of labor can be reduced by eliminating superfluous process elements, by simplifying proceedings, as well as by comprehensive restructuring measures.

Organizational deficits, arisen from a insufficient process orientation of the library, particularly become visible by the analysis of the following relationship: a) sub-processes assigned to the individual cost centers and b) the main processes created by linking sub-processes across cost centers.

- A main process is made up of sub-processes coming from heterogeneous functional centers. Such a main process does not show an emphasis within a single organizational unit, its work steps are fragmented. An example for this is the processing of electronic document orders shown in *figure 1*, which runs through four cost centers. The consolidation of the sub-processes involved into an independent business center that bears the undivided responsibility for the results, is reasonable as a optimization measure.

- A cost center shares its sub-processes with a large number of different main processes. The cost center does not show a coherent task profile. Its process contributions should be taken over by the functional centers primarily responsible for each main process given.

- The activity analysis reveals sub-processes that can not be assigned to any of the library's essential main processes. Those are services that are not related to the core business of the library. They are „nice to have", but from the users' perspective only have a marginal value at the most. Therefore, they should be examined especially critically in regards to their resource requirement (e.g. acquisitions in subjects that aren't taught at the university).

- A main process is characterized by a disproportionately high portion of sub-processes. The sub-processes require little capacities and correspondingly little costs. This is an indicator for a greatly splintered and interface-intensive service. A restructuring of the main processes, e.g. by the combination of sub-processes, should be considered (cf. Niemand 1996, 107).

- A main process is made up of an excessively large number of sub-processes that are all indispensable for the service production. As a rule, the business procedure is overloaded with variants, special cases, and exceptional rules. An example would be the processing of electronic media and other non-book-materials together with the regular course of business. The formation of an independent process for special cases should be considered, according to the motto: „Two simple business processes are better than one complex one."

- The main process is geared for the most complicated processing case. Thereby it is oversized for the majority of the cases. This fact is known as process-fit. It occurs, for instance, when every media going through the business procedure is indiscriminately presented to the subject librarians, although only a limited portion needs to be subject indexed. Setting up different process variants suggests itself. This leads to a reduction of processing time for the simple standard case (cf. Kieninger 1994, 245).

- A main process is constructed of sub-processes that are only partially DP-based or that work with different DP-systems. This requires additional working time, for instance, by repetitive data assessment and counter-check of data.

The implementation of known optimization potentials leads to a diminished resource requirement of the sub-processes and of the main processes. The capacities released are then, for instance, available for use in bottleneck areas. They can also be employed for the construction of a new service offer. A few examples out of the practical experience of University and Regional Library of Münster:

- In the title approach, proofreading descriptive entries took up 770 annual employee hours, the mailbox interaction took up 200 annual hours. Thus altogether, 0.65 employee years were tied up with follow-up work and routine checks. Those, however, are only of a marginal benefit to the title approach. By limiting the controlling to difficult titles, a half of a manpower could be „saved" and transferred to the service area „retrospective cataloging".

- The large amount of time required for conventional guided tours through the library, which has been known about for a long time, is made tangible by the activity analysis: The preparation and execution of a guided tour takes an average of 188 minutes and costs 291 DM (cf. *figure 9*). Optimization measures have been introduced that aim at offering shorter schooling modules for different purposes. The capacities released are going to be employed to support internet-based information services.

- The administrational activities of the local loans of two project libraries were compared (managing the fee register, keeping statistics, etc.). A capacity requirement of a half of an employee year in one case, and two employee years in the other case were revealed, whereby the organizational structure of both loan sites are similar. Without a comparing activity analysis, the need for optimization would have remained unknown. At the same time the process execution of the more efficient library can show concrete alternative courses of action.

- The execution of conventional inter-library borrowing ties up 13.4 employee years. The portion of processes directly dealing with the loan circulation, however, lies at only 3.9 employee years. The remaining 9.5 employee years are taken up exclusively by the holdings check. The staff costs to be rated for this sub-process amount to 888,047 DM. The following optimization measures were introduced: drastic reduction of checking the bibliographical data filled in by the user and of checking the location, promotion for electronic delivery services, improvement of the user advisements regarding inter-library requests. The capacities released here over the medium term are going to be used to strengthen the reference services.

- The analysis for the cost center „computing services" in University and Regional Library shows that only 15% of the available staff capacity participate in the DP-technical support activities of the library's employees. This result confirms the complaint articulated in-house about insufficient DP-support. An employee hired for the Computing Service department was to correct the deficit mentioned above by redefining his tasks.

- Clear differences in the business organization could be determined in the three North-Rhein-Westfalian regional libraries when activity based costing was carried out in order to evaluate of the personnel and materials requirements. For instance, the processing time for legal deposit monographs was between thirty and ninety minutes. Setting up a team for process optimization to develop uniform standard procedures for regional library task seems useful.

If the optimization strategies presented are executed thoroughly and continually in all service areas, they often result in a significant efficiency increase of the process sequences investigated. If, for instance, 3.5 employee years are necessary for acquisition and title approach of 7,000 legal deposit copies before the optimization of the sub-processes involved, only 2 employee years are necessary to accomplish that process volume after restructuring and process streamlining. Thus, the capacity requirement of the process sinks through optimization measures; that means that less staff and other resources are needed for its execution. The process optimization thus generates overcapacity, in the example a surplus of 1.5 employee years. Thereby, idle-capacity costs and idle time occur. The improvement of the process procedure causes the original resources no longer to be optimal (cf. Friedl 1997, 126).

The adjustment of the resources to the changed need can be done in two different ways. On the one hand, the emerging overcapacity can be taken from the optimized process and be redirected to other work areas or new service offers. This leads to a reduction of the costs to be rated for the process analyzed and correspondingly to a reduction of the process cost rates. For instance, processing legal deposit media caused costs of 300,000 DM before the optimization, which through the deduction of 1.5 employees sinks to 200,000 DM. Given 7,000 cost driver units, this means a reduction of the process cost rate from 43 DM to 29 DM. Thus, a cost reduction is attained for the process while keeping the same activity.

On the other hand, however, the increase in process efficiency can be used to raise the intensity of searching and collecting. In that case, the original resources of the service area remain and are employed for an increase in the activity quantity. As a result, the costs do indeed not lessen, however, the process cost rates doubtlessly do, due to the rise in the cost driver units rendered. If, for instance, 9,000 titles per year instead of 7,000 are processed, the process cost rate sinks from 43 DM to 33 DM. As a result a rise in activity is obtained without a rise in costs. Thereby, an improvement of the cost situation in the process area to be optimized is achieved.

Thus, the alternative options that can be decided for are an increase in productivity without a rise in costs or a cost reduction without a curtailment of activity. They are shown in *figure 11*. The illustration clearly shows that optimization measures by themselves are still not accompanied by an improvement of the cost situation of the processes. Due to the high fixed-cost portion, changes in the resource requirement do not lead to cost changes until the existing staff and material have been adjusted to the changed need. In other words, the increase of efficiency has to be accompanied by deliberate decisions for the reallocation or for the reduction of resources in order to become cost effective. If those decisions are not made, resource overcapacities emerges and thereby inevitably idle-capacity costs and idle time.

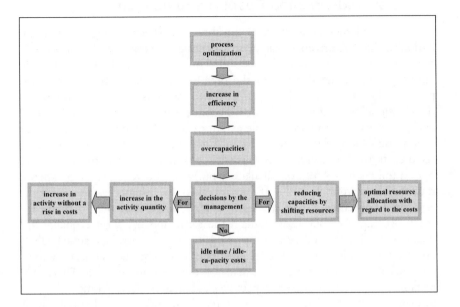

Fig. 11: The Cost Effects of Optimization Strategies.

As was explained in chapter 4.5, every process possesses a certain achievement potential, which is expressed by the cost driver units of that process. In the example given above, the activity capability of the process „processing legal deposit media" lays at 7,000 media units before the optimization, and at 9,000 afterwards. The achievement potential of a process is the amount of available process executions that can be rendered with a given resources and a certain process organization. The resources made available for the process execution are, as a general rule, to be sized in such a way that neither overcapacities nor shortages arise. An overcapacities of resources exists, for instance, when the process of legal deposit media provision is designed for 9,000 units, but only 8,000 relevant titles are published. Besides process optimization, another important task of cost management is the demand-oriented adjustment of capacities, especially of the staff capacity. This is necessary for a cost-optimal resource allocation. The measures to be taken here, which naturally are preferably to be directed at processes already optimized, are sketched in the following chapter.

5.2 Demand-Oriented Resource Allocation

In the implementation phase of the library's cost accounting, the determination of the cost drivers of the processes should be done on the basis of actual values from the accounting period. Those can generally be taken from existing statistical databases. For the sake of rapid achievement of the first partial results, the ascertainment effort for the analysis of the cost drivers can thus be significantly limited. The actual production amount of a process, however, often varies to a considerable extent over the periods, for instance, due to a modification of the service offers. Since the costs are for the most part fixed costs, the fluctuation leads to process cost rates that vary from period to period (cf. chapter 4.5). For calculatory purposes, however, varying expense ratios are only limitedly useful. If they are taken, for instance, as a basis for the assessment of remuneration, this leads to a frequent change of price, while for the most part the total costs remain the same and the service quality unchanged. Such a procedure incomprehensible to the user. The actual values are also unsuitable when, in the framework of make/buy decisions, cost comparisons with private suppliers are made on the basis of unit costs. This is, for instance, the case with the retrospective cataloging projects. Comparable values can only be attained, if the activity rendered under normal conditions is considered. The ascertainment of normed cost driver values, however, is indispensable, for cost-oriented capacity management. Given constant resources, different capacity utilization rates cause idle-capacity costs to the same extent that the actual amount remains below the normal activity of the process area being considered.

After concluding the initial phase of the cost accounting, the actual value of the cost drivers should be complimented successively, beginning with the library's core processes. The cost drivers should be complimented by values that, considering the given staff and material, describe realizable amounts. This amount denotes the so-called normal capacity of a process. The normal capacity does not describe how many cost driver units were performed in the past accounting period or are probably to be expected in the coming period. It rather describes how many units can be performed with the available resources (cf. Cooper/Kaplan 1999, 78). In other words, it is a matter of a target value and not actual nor anticipated data.

To ascertain these values, the first step is to undertake a comparative analysis of the cost driver values achieved in the past. Example: With constant provision of the process „acquiring and processing textbook material" with staff and materials at University and Regional Library Münster, the following case figures are the results for the cost driver „number of acquired volumes":

1994 - 5,869; 1995 - 4,564; 1996 - 7,252; 1997 - 8,251; 1998 - 8,051. The time series data offer the first indication as to which range of values the normal capacity to be shown could fall into. However, these should not be gained by a simple average of the actual amounts performed from period to period. The known phenomenon of „cost slack" militates against that, in other words, the fact that the resources available are seldom really used sparingly to accomplish the task with optimal efficiency. The extent of cost slack always becomes visible when peak demands or withdrawals of resources can be managed without activity deficits or with only a negligible activity deficit. „The flexibility then perceivable in the system ‚company' can only be explained by unrecognized ‚qualitative' and ‚quantitative' reserves, without the existence of which an adaptability of that kind could not happen" (Schoenfeld 1997, 433). It is thus not at all unrealistic to presume that the normal capacity of each given process analyzed is in the upper area of the period values ascertained. Therefore, the reference values gained from time series analysis should be corrected in a second step by activity estimates. The estimates are to be obtained in coordination with the employees executing the process as well as, in certain cases, with targets set by unit heads. It especially needs to be examined, whether and to what degree the peak workload of the time series is connected with the postponement of less important work, high proportions of overtime, increasing absenteeism, etc. This, as a rule, points to an overloading of the resources. In the case of the example considered, the normal capacity was fixed, in agreement with the employees responsible for the process, at 8,000 cost driver units annually. This number represents a feasible norm for the cost driver amount for the given resources.

According to the calculation carried out in chapter 4.7, the process „acquiring and processing textbook material" causes costs of 208,000 DM and ties up 4,660 annual hours (3.2 employee years). By dividing the costs by the normal capacity of the process, an expense ratio of 26 DM per processed media unit is calculated. This value denotes the target process cost rate. That means that the process activity rendered under normal conditions causes a unit cost of 26 DM. Correspondingly, the quotient of the employee annual hours made available for the process execution and the normal capacity is the time required per cost driver unit (35 min.). Since this value was calculated on the basis of the normal capacity, it can be considered as the standard time for a single process execution. With the help of these values, the resource requirement or resource overcapacity can be calculated. If for some reason the estimated number of media to be acquired in the coming accounting period is only 6000, the staff requirement of 3,500 annual employee hours (6,000 x

35 min.) can be calculated by multiplying this amount by the standard time. This value describes the staff capacity needed to render the process quantity planned for. 4,660 annual employee hours actually available for the process execution represent the available staff capacity. The quotient of the manpower requirement and the staff supply gives the capacity utilization of the process, which is 75% (3,500 / 4,660 x 100). Thus, an idle time proportion of 25% (= 1,165 hrs.) is obtained. Correspondingly, costs of the resources actually needed are amounting to 156,000 DM (6,000 x 26 DM). This is calculated by multiplying the planned process quantity by the target process cost rate. The actual costs of 208,000 DM represent the costs of the available resources. Analogous to the calculation of the idle time, idle-capacity costs of 52,000 are accordingly the result. This denotes the costs of the resources that are held ready in an accounting period, but are not used. This calculation can be brought down to the simple formula processes available = processes used + surplus capacities (Cooper/Kaplan 1995, 50).

The same calculation can obviously be carried out to determine the resource shortage and correspondingly the staff requirement needed. If, for instance, a cost driver amount of 11,000 accessions a year has been planned, a staff requirement of 6,420 annual hours (4.3 employee years) can be calculated on the basis of the standard time for the processing of one media unit (35 min.). Given 3.2 available employee years for the process, a resource shortage of around one employee year results. Looking at the figures presented in the example, the core problem of cost management for service institutions becomes visible once more. Since the costs are for the most part fixed cost with a medium to long term commitment period, changes in the cost driver amount do not automatically lead to a cost change. Only the insignificant portion of variable costs are affected by each given capacity utilization rate. Changes in the process quantity merely effects a change in the resource requirement. The extent of the requirement can be exactly determined with the help of the data delivered by the activity based costing. Thus, for the process „acquiring and processing textbook material", with a process activity 25% less that the normal capacity, a surplus capacity of 1,165 hours or 0,75 employee year is calculated. The decrease in the cost driver amount thus signals a cost reduction potential for the analyzed process. This, however, can only be actualized permissively, that means by a deliberate reallocation of the surplus resources or by their reduction. If the decision to redetermine the resources is not made, idle-capacity costs and idle time arise and thereby cost inefficiencies.

The extent to what necessary interventions into the available resource stock can be made depends upon the concrete operational basic conditions on site. Ranked among this group are, for instance, legal aspects, contract periods, as well as especially the qualification level of the employees. Beyond that, it is to be taken into account that the potential factors of the service production (personnel, assets) are indivisible. Thus, they cannot continually be adjusted to the given capacity utilization rate (cf. Backhaus/Funke 1997, 41). The change in the activity amount first has to exceed or fall below certain marginal values to make an adjustment of the resources possible or necessary. Looking at the process „acquiring and processing textbook material", a reduction of utilization by 300 units would scarcely make a redeployment of staff possible, just as little as an overload of the same amount would justify an additional staff requirement. As opposed to that, the activity increase to 11,000 units would compellingly require the provision of additional resources.

Calculations on the basis of target expense ratios allow the degree of cost efficiency of a service process to become transparent. Therefore, they are to be used in every case where the user of the library is drawn upon for the financing of those services. The case presently most important is the remuneration assessment for the use of electronic document delivery services. University libraries, as a general rule, have to ensure the free and general access to scientific information. Because of this, it has to be made sure that services with a remuneration obligation are calculated exclusively on the basis of resources used in a cost optimal way and are thereby the services are offered at a most reasonable price. In particular, burdening the user with costs that do not arise because of the service, but rather by inefficiencies of the service production is to be avoided (cf. von Zwehl 1997, 208f.).

If, for instance, a business center set up for document delivery services is operated with staff and materials designed for 30,000 orders annually, then, given assumed costs of 240,000 DM, a process cost rate of 8 DM is calculated. This would have to be calculated as remuneration. If only 23,000 orders are received on an average each period, this will mean a capacity utilization rate of 77%. Correspondingly a 185,000 DM used-capacity costs proportion of the total cost and a idle-capacity costs proportion of 55,000 DM are calculated. The library can try to dump the total costs in full amount onto the user by setting the price per delivered document to 10.50 DM. In that case, however, the remuneration to be paid, contains a hidden idle-capacity costs proportion. Thus, the users of the delivery service not only reimburse the costs of the orders that the library really obtained, but also the costs of the orders not obtained. Instead of dumping the costs of inefficient service production onto the user, the library should rather try to reduce the oversized resources of the delivery service corresponding to the demand. One option is to reassess the employee capacity needed. Alternatively, the demand could be increased by shortening the delivery times or through intensified promotion in order to maintain or even decrease the original price.

With this simplified example once again the decision-oriented approach of the activity based costing becomes clear. Whereas cost type accounting and cost center accounting each merely distribute the occurring costs, the activity based costing does an analysis of the process efficiency and thereby the cost efficiency of the service production. At the same time, it allows the break down of the library processes into their constituent sub-process sequences. Thus, discovered inefficiencies can be followed down into the microstructure of the service production and can be purposefully eliminated.

The calculation examples presented up until now deal exclusively with yearly planning and decision situations. Changes in the basic conditions that occur at short notice (budget cuts, project tasks, special funds, etc.) often require, however, a reallocation of existing resources within that year. *Figure 12* shows, by means of a simple example, to what extent the activity based costing can support quick capacity adjustments in order to dispose resources in a cost-optimal way.

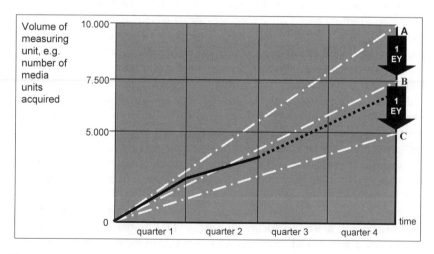

Fig. 12: Steerage Within the Year

Shown are three scenarios concerning the number of cost driver units to be rendered within a year by the process „acquiring and processing textbook material". Scenario A deals with 10,000, B with 7,500, and C with 5,000 planned accessions. The standard time for the acquiring and processing a media unit calculated above is 35 minutes. Corresponding to this time, a capacity requirement of 5,800 hours is calculated for the planned process quantity A (about four employee years), for B a requirement of three employee years, and for C two. Thus, there is a difference of one employee year between scenario A and scenario B, and between B and C, respectively. It is then assumed that at the beginning of an accounting period an activity quantity of 10,000 accessions are planned so that the process is equipped with four employee years plus the necessary materials. For cost-oriented capacity management it is crucial to be able to take adjustment action within the accounting period in case of a divergence of the actualized process quantity from the planned quantity. If, for instance, 2,000 accessions less than the planned quantity are only mentioned in the annual financial statement, the idle-capacity costs and idle time proportion (35 Min x 2,000 = 1,170 hrs.) can only be documented, but no longer be influenced.

Therefore, a mandatory quarterly report about the actualized process quantity is assumed in the example. It is also assumed that the activity development up to the middle of the year takes the course represented by the black line in *figure 12*. Several things can be responsible for this development, for instance, a inadequate offer of new publications, cost-cutting measures, or budget shift at short notice. In view of the existing information, it might be predicted that the annual process quantity will not exceed the value of 7,500 units, which holds true for scenario B. A half of an employee year can therefore be taken from the process at the end of the second quarter and can be reallocated to another functional center. Correspondingly, the process „acquiring and processing textbook material" is to be relieved in regards to the costs, while the center reinforced with staff is to be burdened. Idle times and idle-capacity costs that would have inevitably occurred from a retrospective view can thus be avoided for the most part by a capacity utilization analysis carried out in intervals of less than a year.

The disposable staff capacity ascertained, however, at first only represents a purely mathematical figure. The extent to what redirections actually take place, depends upon the concrete corporate basic conditions. As explained in chapter 4.5., the half of an employee year ascertained in the example as being disposable is not completely available. The process „acquiring and processing textbook material" also comprises sub-processes that are not affected by the cost driver *number of acquired volumes*. The sub-processes „placing orders" and „cataloging", for instance, are assigned to the cost driver *number of acquired titles*. The capacity requirement of these processes, however, does not necessarily sink with the amount of media units processed. The requirement only declines, if there is a decrease in the number of titles and not only a lessened number of multiple copies. Since the former is not likely in the case of textbook material, the real resource disposition is probably lower than what the calculation indicated.

The option of a cost management of service processes, shown here by means of a simple example, will noticeably gain significance for libraries in the course of budget globalization. Resource utilization is freed more and more from the restrictions of the traditional item-economy. Corresponding with the proceedings of this process, the library is, on the one hand, able to conduct resource planning for several periods. On the other hand it also gets the chance of reacting flexibly to short notice changes of the users' needs and of managing the new service demands. Activity based costing supports these options by evaluating the changed resource requirements in regards to capacity and costs. It thus makes the quick reallocation of available staff and materials possible.

5.3   Raising the Cost Flexibility

The previous chapters have pointed out the basic instruments of cost management for service institutions with intensive fixed costs: the continual optimization of the service process and the thorough demand-oriented allocation of the resources available. It became evident that changes in the capacity unitization rate, i.e. an increase or decrease in the cost driver amount, do not automatically bring about cost changes. Only the marginal portion of variable costs changes with each given capacity utilization rate. The influencing and structuring of the costs always requires a decision from the library management to redispose the available resources. By the exemplary calculations new insights were given into the problems arising with fixed costs when implementing cost type accounting. At least on the steering level of the sub-processes and the main processes, the library costs are not fixed, but rather controllable for the most part: Every intervention into the available resources leads directly to a change in the costs and process cost rates. It is not in the least a matter of simply relieving the processes „giving the resources" and burdening the activities „taking the resources". The measures taken in process optimization and in capacity management can extend the library's scope considerably, it they are carried out thoroughly. It is possible to either raise the activity volume of a process without increasing the resource requirement, or to shrink the demand for resources while keeping a constant activity amount. As was shown in chapter 5.1, both alternatives lead to an improvement of the cost efficiency. Especially the second option is due to stagnating or receding budgets important for libraries. Capacities can be gained to offer new service, especially in the area of digital information services.

To the extent that university libraries can manage their funds autonomously, they obtain additional usage alternatives for the capacities known to be in excess. Since the staff costs represents the cost factor crucial for steering purposes, the scenario of a completely global budget is especially interesting. The position chart would be replaced by a blanket personnel budget (cf. exemplarily Volkert 1996). In this context, the staff over-covering can not be only re-planned, but can also be reduced by natural fluctuations. The resulting budget relief can then be used for investments, for instance, in information technologies or for reinforcing the media budget. The cost effect of those interventions can be broken down to the process level and reveal, for instance, to a changed relation of the staff costs of a process to the depreciation charges.

Not only within the company the costs of main processes and sub-process represent the main steerage determinants. In the framework of budget agreements and service agreements, it is the costs of processes (the annual costs of document delivery services, of loans, etc.) and process cost rates (the costs of an online inquiry, a schooling, an advisement, etc.) by which the library is measured on the part of the decision makers. Those values are also drawn upon to compare the library with other libraries and with private suppliers. Process-optimizing and capacity-managing measures support the cost-effective structuring of the service offers and improve the library's chances of securing more funds from the universities limited budget..

In order to optimally use the freedom gained in financially autonomous fund management, the library has to reduce the hindrance to cuts coming from fixed costs in the long run. Those costs can be cut, for instance, by giving preference to fixed-term contracts as opposed to a contract for an unlimited period, or by leasing assets instead of buying them (cf. Backhaus/Funke 1997, 40ff.). By shortening the commitment period of fixed costs, an increase in cost manageability is attained. This facilitates the adjustment to the fluctuation in utilization and to new demands for service - an essential factor, considering the enormous tempo of innovation in the information sector. The options for the cost-optimal structuring of service offers introduced in the preceding chapters also show that the missed opportunities of increasing the efficiency is not to be excused by referring to the dominance of fixed costs in the library's costs. Allegedly „fixed" staff costs oftentimes indicate insufficient willingness to take advantage of known opportunities of efficiency improvement. The process-optimizing measures could have just as well have been left undone. If, on the contrary, steering instruments are thoroughly employed, significant gains in capacity can be obtained. With the help of these, the expanding gulf between growing tasks and tighter finances can be decreased a bit.

The reallocation of the resources made available constantly demands an overall consideration of the services offered by the library, if it is not to exhaust itself in taking ad hoc measures,. In cooperation with the university heads, the library has to develop a strategic perspective that answers questions like

- Which of the services belong to the indispensable core business?

- Which services are to be expanded, which are to be reduced?

- How will tasks be weighted in a multi-year budgeting?

The production of a product portfolio suggests itself as a frame of reference for a long-term oriented planning of resource utilization. Therewith, the strategic positioning of the library's services can be made transparent easily (for the possibilities of use of the portfolio technique originally developed by Boston Consulting Group cf. Günther 1999). As *figure 13* exemplarily shows, a four field matrix is constructed. The x-axis depicts the current intensity of use of the library's products („service demand"), whereas the y-axis displays the forecasted or planned product demand („strategic importance").

The size of the circle describing the library's service marks the staff capacity taken up and thereby the determining cost factor. Services having a higher strategic significance but that currently still have a lower demand (e.g. electronic document delivery services) make up the library's „rising generation of services", to which resources have to be increasingly made available. Services with current and future intensity of demand are the „stars" in the product portfolio with a correspondingly high capacity requirement and - with good reason - a high proportion of costs. Products with a traditionally higher demand, but with a usually decreasing one for the future (e.g. conventional interlibrary loans), characterize service areas that resources can be taken out of over the medium term. This holds even more for the current and probably also future weakly demanded offers (e.g. collection building in subjects that are being phased out). If need be, those services should be taken out of the catalog of offers.

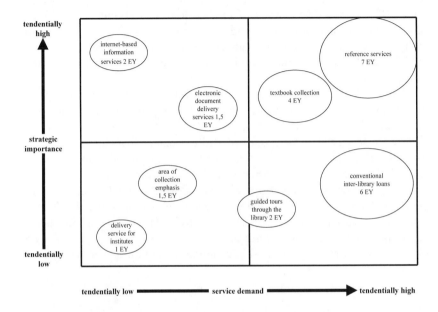

Fig. 13: A Portfolio of Selected Library Services

The weighted products can be juxtaposed with a target portfolio that represents the targeted service profile of the library, approximately for the year 2003. The juxtaposition of the actual portfolio with the target portfolio shows resource over-covering and resource requirements which are to be expected. It thereby sets the direction of the capacity balancing in the portfolio, for instance, by eliminating services having a weak demand and correspondingly by reinforcing the rising generation of products. In principle, the services offered by the library should be located as much as possible in the three outer quadrant. The field of less demanded and strategically insignificant products should remain unoccupied as much as possible. The rising generation of products characterizes the library's future shape, the „stars" determine its current appearance from the users view, and the remaining products represent basic services of decreasing relevance in the long run.

Product portfolios show what the library's core tasks are, what its strengths and weaknesses are, and especially shows whether the available resources are primarily used for the strategically most significant service processes. The informative content of the portfolio is even increased when the process dimensions costs, time, and quality are taken equally into consideration. Costs and expense ratios, capacity requirements and processing times (which already represent important indicators of quality), as well as cost driver amounts can be gathered from the activity based costing.

If these data are complemented with the results of a systematic performance appraisal, a differentiated judgment of the products mentioned in the portfolio is possible (cf. Poll/teBoekhorst 1998, 37). For instance, the product „reference service" can be described and evaluated by its annual costs (e.g. 420,000 DM), its capacity requirement (e.g. 4.7 employee years), its output (e.g. 85,000 reference questions answered), and its success rate (e.g. 60% reference questions answered correctly). Such Portfolios could then be used in benchmarking projects or be used as a basis of service agreements and budget agreements with the university heads. Activity based costing and activity based management in this way become components of a comprehensive controlling of the university's provision of literature and information.

6 Software Support for the Cost Management: LIBRARYMANAGER

The efficient execution of the cost accounting requires the employment of a powerful software tool usable in flexible ways. LIBRARYMANAGER, a Windows based software described in the following, supports the buildup of both the conventional cost type and cost center accounting as well as the activity based costing within the specific organizational framework of university libraries. LIBRARYMANAGER allows user defined analyses or, parallel accountings by means of independently definable cost accounting objects. Over 70 reports provide for an informative cost and capacity reporting.

The installation has the following computer system requirements:

Computer System Requirements
Operating systems:

- Windows 95/98, Windows NT 4.0, or later.

Hardware:

- 90 MHz Pentium processor or equivalent
- 64 MB of RAM.
- 30 MB Hard Disk Space
- A CD-ROM drive and mouse.
- A 15" Monitor (17" is recommended). With the help of the control panel, at the least a resolution of 800 x 600 pixel (1024 x 768 is recommended) and 256 simultaneous colors (recommended is high color, 16 bit) should be set. The software layout was optimized for a high number of colors.

Network:

- In a network, LIBRARYMANAGER cost modules can be simultaneously processed by several users / clients. LIBRARAYMANAGER needs to be installed on each Client PC. An installation on a server is not enough.

Installation / Uninstallation
The installation and uninstallation is carried out by going through the following steps:

1.	LIBRARYMANAGER was generated during a project sponsored by Deutsche Forschungsgemeinschaft. The purchaser of this book may install and use LIBRARYMANAGER. Hereby, a financial usage on the part of the purchaser is not allowed. The authors do not accept liability for the general operativeness of the software.

2. Execute the SETUP.EXE file on the CD-ROM either by double-clicking it in Windows-Explorer or by using the function „Run - D:\SETUP.EXE" in the Windows start menu.

3. The installation program then leads you through the installation process and asks for the following particulars: a) the target directory and b) the program folder for LIBRARYMANAGER.

4. The installation routines for the time logging module are found in the directory „ZeitErf" on the CD-ROM. To install the time logging module, execute the file SETUP.EXE found in this directory.

5. For an installation of LIBRARYMANAGER on the Windows NT 4.0 operating system, several system configurations require that the NT Service Pack 4 from the directory „NT4SP4\i386\update" is installed as the very first thing. In those cases, LIBRARYMANAGER's installation routine draws your attention to that. You would need to run the file „sp6i386.exe".

6. To uninstall, double-click the symbol „software" in the control panel.(The control panel is found in the menu „settings" in the Windows start menu.) In the dialog, either the entry „LIBRARYMANAGER" or „LM time logging module" is to be selected. Afterwards, click the button „Delete"

After the installation of LIBRARYMANAGER and the time logging module, symbols for calling up a program are both in the program folders defined during the installation as well as on the Windows desktop. LIBRARYMANAGER is ran by double-clicking the program icon.

To ensure the operativeness of the software, the regional setting in the Windows control panel (tab: numbers) need to be specified as follows: The decimal separator needs to be a point (.) and the thousand separator as comma (,).

The construction of LIBRARYMANAGER exactly follows the accounting model described in the handbook. The user should therefore be able to manage the software without any difficulty. LIBRARYMANAGER can be used for the production, processing, and presentation of cost models. A cost model consist of cost types, cost centers, sub-processes, main processes, business processes, and other cost accounting objects. In the LIBRARYMANAGER's installation directory, a fictive example model „UBDEMO" is found. It supports understanding the creation of a cost model as described in the following. *Figure 14* represents the LIBRARYMANAGER's working screen after loading a cost model:

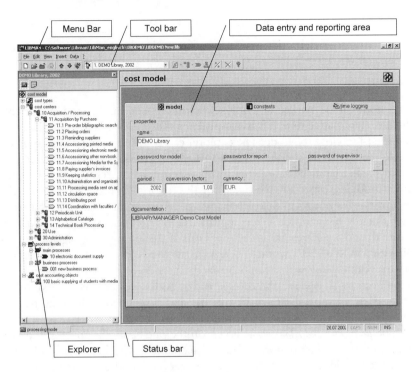

Fig. 14: LIBRARYMANAGER's Working screen

In order to facilitate the data entry, the *status bar* presents context-sensitive information about the cost model. From the status bar in *figure 14* it can be seen, for example, that 100% of the staff capacity of the cost center *11 subject librarians* was allocated to its sub-processes, thus the data entry is completed. A highlighted entry on the status bar „CAPS" in the lower right of the figure would mean that the capitalization mode of the PC-keyboard is active. „NUM" signalizes the activation of the numeric keyboard and „INS" the activation of the text insert mode instead of the overwrite mode. The *explorer* reflects the hierarchical structure of the cost model in the form of a tree structure. By using this tree, the user can navigate through the cost model by mouse click. In a new cost model, the following nodes, or as the case may be, objects, represented as symbols, are found in the explorer:

- cost types,

- cost centers (with sub-processes to be set up),

- process levels (with main processes and business processes to be set up), as well as

- other cost accounting objects.

A node can be marked by a mouse click and opened and closed by a double click. An alternative to that is to simply click the [+] symbol to open the node and the [-] to close the node. The explorer can be taken out of its mooring on the left edge of the LIBRARYMANAGER's working screen, moved, and made smaller to make more room available for the on-screen indicators for other modules, especially for those for the reports. In order to take out the explorer, it is enough to double-click its title bar. An alternative to that is to click the title bar and, while keeping the left mouse button pressed, to drag it out to the docking area, in other words out of the left or right edge of the LIBRARYMANAGER's working screen. Afterwards, the explorer is displayed in a moveable window that can be resized. In order to redock the explorer, the steps need to be done in the reverse order. A double click on the explorer's title bar, or a simple click on the title bar and subsequently dragging the explorer back into the border area of the working screen moors it.

The *data entry and report mode* serves, on the one hand, the entry of the data relevant for the construction of the cost accounting. On the other hand, it enables the presentation of reports. It depends on the nodes selected on the explorer tree, which data entry mask, or report open up in this part of the working screen. In order to resize the explorer, as well as the data entry mode and report mode, the dividing line between the both screen areas can be moved with the mouse. To do that, you need to place the mouse pointer on the dividing line, press the left mouse button, and then pull the window to the desired size. Besides that, a lot of the tabs in the data entry area contain a documentation field into which the compiler can put individual references and complimentary information regarding the procedure (e.g. responsibility, instructions for examination, reasons for implementing a sub-process, or comments concerning time logging).

LIBRARYMANAGER is steered by functions. Functions are arranged in the working screen in so-called menus on the *menu bar* and *tool bar*. Each menu is provided with a button on the menu bar and tool bar (cf. *figure 14*). Examples for functions are „generate new cost model“, „open cost model“, and „create new cost type“. Menus can be selected with a key combination of [Alt] or [AltGr] and a letter underlined in the menu name, or alternatively by a mouse click. LIBRARYMANAGER's tool bars are equipped with the following buttons, which can identically be found again in the menus.

Standard Tool Bar	Context Tool Bar
☐ Create New Cost Model	☐ Create New Time Logging Database
☞ Open Cost Model	☞ Open Time Logging Database
☐ Close Active Cost Model	✓ Recalculate Staff Capacity Shares
☐ Print Table or Report	☐ Export Data: Time Logging and Reports
⇧ Element above	☐ Import Time Logging Data
⇩ Element down	◄ Show First Record / Report Page
☐ Sorting Mode On / Off	◄ Show Previous Record / Report Page
☐ Hide or Show Explorer	► Show Next Record / Report Page
☐ Create New Cost Type	►◄ Show Last Record / Report Page
☐ Create New Cost Center	✗ Delete Record
☐ Create New Process	☐ Create New Constant
☐ Create New Cost Accounting Object	☐ Create New Employee
% Percental Cost Type Increase	☐ Create New Operating Resource
✗ Delete the Node Selected in the Explorer	☐ Create New Allocation Key
☐ Help	☐ Create New Cost Driver
Explorer Tool Bar	☐ Modify Cost Driver or Allocation Key
☐ Switch to Processing Mode	☐ Enter Filtering Criteria
☐ Switch to Report Mode	☐ Filter Records According to Criteria
☐ Report Only Budget Affecting Costs	☐ Delete Filtering Criteria

Fig. 15: LIBRARYMANAGER's Tool Bars' Buttons

Figure 15 differentiates between the buttons of different tool bars. The standard tool bar is always visible - as long as the user does not make it invisible. Whether the context tool bars is visible or invisible, is always dependent upon each given processing relationship. In addition to the buttons shown in *figure 15*, the standard tool bar contains a combo-box for selecting a cost model (cf. *figure 14*). The combo-box allows the user to switch back and forth between the different cost models that have been opened. This way of processing and representing a large number of cost models was chosen instead of including every single cost model on the explorer tree in order to avoid an overly complex tree representation.

The explorer's tool bar contains two buttons to switch between the processing mode and the report mode. In the processing mode, the user can enter or modify the data of a cost model using entry masks. The report mode displays reports about the cost model. By right-clicking a node on the explorer tree, self-explanatory context menus appear. In case a function is not available in the current processing context, the corresponding button is left gray. Which function is connected with a button is found out by moving the mouse pointer to the button. An information box appears, which briefly explains the respective function.

Defining a cost model

In order to generate a new and empty cost model, the corresponding [create a new cost model] button (cf. *figure 15*) is to be used. As a result, a dialog box „save as ..." appears, into which the user is to give a path and file name for the new cost model's database. LIBRARYMANAGER automatically adds the extension „.LIB" to the file name.

All data entries and changes are immediately saved in the database. That is why the standard tool bar does not contain a [save] button; thus a saving initiated by the user is not necessary.

After the creation of a new cost model, the explorer shows the new cost model's nodes on the tree structure. At first the node „model" is marked. In the data entry area, an entry mask belonging to this node opens. It shows tabs to structure the entry elements according to subject matter. For instance, three tabs belong to the entry mask for the „model" node: „model", „constants", and „time logging". The tabs additionally structure the entry elements with group controls.

In the group control „properties", the tab *model* allows for the entry field „name", in which a name of the cost model can be recorded (e.g. ULB Münster), and furthermore the entry fields „model password", „report password", „supervisors password", „period" (e.g. 1999), conversion factor (e.g. 1), and „currency" (e.g. EUR).

New passwords are not defined in the entry field, but in a dialog box. The dialog box is called up by clicking the [...] buttons next to the entry fields. If an existing password is to be changed, it is to be entered into the corresponding field before the dialog call-up. The model password is asked for before the opening of a cost model, the report password before the change into the report mode described further below, and the supervisor password before the activation of the tab „time logging" as well as before displaying reports containing personal data.

The „conversion factor" and „currency" determine the unit for the costs in the reports. The entered cost values are divided by the conversion factor. A conversion factor of 1,000 and the currency „TEUR" effects, for instance, that the costs are reported in a unit of a thousand EUR.

The entry and post-editing of data with the help of LIBRARYMAN-AGER's entry fields are simplified by certain short cuts. Using the enter key or tabulator key, the next entry field is activated. The key F2 deletes the content of a entry field completely. ESC cancels the data changes, or as the case may be, discontinues the entry. From the numerical entry fields, which for example serve the cost entry, the space key can be used to have a *calculator* pop up. This can then be used for calculation and automated transfer of the calculation results into the entry field that the call-up was done from. An initializing of the calculator is done in certain cases with a number entered earlier in the entry field. The basic kinds of calculation: addition, subtraction, multiplication, and division, are supported. By clicking the [equals] button, the calculation process is triggered. By clicking the [OK] button, the calculation results are transferred to the entry field.

In a list field, the tab *constants* contains a list of constants necessary for the calculation of certain cost types and capacity values. The first two constants of this list are given cannot be deleted. The „net working time in hours per year" specifies the employee year (for example 1,476 hours). The „work weeks per year for assistants" indicates the net work weeks (e.g. 48) to be performed by the assistants annually, that means without taking the vacation weeks into account.

The value of a constant selected from the list field can be changed in the entry field. A new constant is created by clicking the corresponding symbol (cf. *figure 15*). Its name is to be entered into the corresponding field. User-defined constants can be deleted by clicking the corresponding button on the context tool bar (cf. *figure 15*). An example for user-defined constants is a prevailing interest rate of 0.06. Before changing the designation or the value of a constant, it is to be marked in the list by a mouse click.

The tab *time logging* is explained further down in connection with the time logging module.

Defining Cost Types

When the node „cost types" is marked on the explorer tree, a tab having the same name is displayed that shows a data sheet. With the aid of that data sheet, the number, the name, and the documentation of the cost types already entered can be modified. To do that, a person either clicks the cell to be changed with the mouse, or navigates to the cell by using the arrow keys. The content of the cell can be processed both by either clicking the place to be changed with the mouse, or by simply beginning with the data entry. After a data sheet has been activated, the data content in the data sheet can be printed out by mouse click with the help of the [print data sheet] button (cf. *figure 15*).

When the node „cost types" is marked, a new cost type can be created by using the corresponding button on the standard tool bar (cf. *figure 15*). Eleven different kinds of cost types, which are described in the following, are available. The type of the new cost type to be made is either to be determined in the dialog, by the user clicking the [make new cost type] button on the standard tool bar, or from a context menu, by the user clicking the arrow next to that button.

A cost type of the type „structure" serves the hierarchization of the cost type accounting. LIBRARYMANAGER allows up to ten levels of hierarchy. Thus, if the node „cost type" is marked, one could, for example, create the new cost type „100 staff costs" of the type „structure". This new cost type would then be attached to the explorer tree below the cost type node. In order to create, for example, the new cost type „110 staff costs, civil servants" on the structural level below that, the user would have to select the node „100 staff costs" and generate a further cost type of the type „structure" which would then be inserted below the node „100 staff costs". With a cost type of the type „structure", only the number (e.g. 100), the name (e.g. staff costs), and a documentation of the cost type can be recorded or, as the case my be, modified.

The entry fields named here are identical with the fields found for cost types of all other types. For this reason, they will not be further mentioned in the explanation of the other types of cost types. Unlike a cost type of the type „structure", a check box is available for cost types of all other types for setting the criterion „budget affective", which is relevant for the cost report. This criterion serves the purpose of making selected cost types visible or invisible in the reports for various analysis objectives. This will considered in greater detail further on in the section „creating reports". Only when the node „cost types" or a node that belongs to a cost type of the type „structure" is marked on the explorer tree, does the possibility exist of creating a new cost type on a level immediately below the marked node. A tab „cost type" lists, in data sheet form, all of the cost types assigned to the structural level selected.

LIBRARYMANAGER presents a choice of four types of staff cost types, namely „staff costs, civil servants", „staff costs, salaried employees", „staff costs, workers", and „staff costs, assistants". For instance, one could click the node „110 staff costs, civil servants" on the explorer tree on, and then create a new cost type „111 staff costs, civil servants, academics" of the type „civil servants" below that node. The entry mask of the staff cost types mentioned here shows two tabs.

The first of the tabs is named after the type of cost type, in other words, is called *civil servants, salaried employees, workers,* or *assistants.* Except for the type „assistants", the cost types require an independent data record for every employee including the name of the employee. For that purpose, a context tool bar appears that has buttons for navigating between the employee data records, as well as for the creation, the deletion, and for the filtering of those data records (cf. *figure 15*).

In the group control „employee", there is an entry field for recording both the employees name and an employee password. The significance of the employee password, which is to be entered analogous to the procedure of recording passwords described above, is explained further on in connection with the time logging model. Further entry fields allow the recording of the positions of an employee (for example a 1 stands for a full-time position, 0.75 for a three-quarter, and 0.5 for a half-time position), and the recording of the number of months that the employee is employed in the library's accounting period. Usually this is 12 months, however, this value can also be lower due to staff fluctuation.

Furthermore, the combo-box „salary group" allows the classification of employees according to their salary group, remuneration group, or wage group. To do that, salary groups need to be defined separately for each type of staff cost type. This is done with the help of the [...] button on the right side next to the combo-box. In the dialog for determining these groups, a data sheet and the buttons [new], [delete], [increase in costs for the groups ...], as well as [close] are found. By clicking [new], a new salary-, remuneration-, or wage group is added to the data sheet. In the data sheet column „salary group", the name of the group can be changed. The annual costs to be assigned to a salary-, remuneration-, or wage group are to be entered into the column with the heading „costs". By using the [delete] button, a group already recorded can be deleted. Beforehand, the group to be deleted is to be marked in the data sheet by clicking it. By clicking the [increase in costs for the groups...] button, an entry mask is made visible, which serves the entry of a percental increment factor with which the cost values of all of the groups shown in the data sheet are adjusted. After determining the percentage increment factor, the [OK] button is to be clicked. This procedure simplifies taking the annual tariff adjustment into consideration in the cost accounting.

The group control „allocation to cost centers" allows the assignment of the employee in process to cost centers on the basis of the annual hours that the employee was active in the respective cost centers. To do that, a cost center affected is to be selected in the combo-box. In the entry field, LIBRARY-

MANAGER suggests the allocation of the „annual hours" not yet assigned. This suggested value is calculated by using the formula: Not yet allocated annual manhours = (constant „net working time in hours per year" x the entry in the text box „position" x the entry in the text box „months employed" / 12) minus the annual hours already allocated to other cost centers.

The value thus ascertained can be diminished manually by the entry of a lower number of annual hours A later alteration of the values in the entry fields „months employed" and „position" causes the affected employee's hourly capacity assigned to one or more cost centers to automatically be adjusted correspondingly to the new value. A later change of the constant value „net working time in hours per year" leads to an adjustment of the hour-related allocation to the cost centers for all employees. In particular cases, it can hereby come to a rounding discrepancy that leads to the employees, previously assigned completely with their manhours to cost centers, now no longer being completely assigned. In that case, the allocation of the employees to the cost centers is to be touched up. By means of the F5 function key, the employee's hourly capacity not already allocated is assigned to the selected cost center, if the cursor is in the entry field „annual hours".

An allocation of employees to the cost centers of course requires for the cost centers to be previously set up with the functions described further down in the section „defining cost centers and sub-processes". In order to avoid a non-productive jumping back and forth during the determining of cost types on the one hand and cost centers on the other hand, it is expedient *to build the cost center structure first and the cost type accounting afterwards.*

The context tool bar contains a button for filtering the employee data records (cf. *figure 15*). With the aid of filter criteria, the number of the data records displayed is reduced. To do that, the user has to determine filter criteria by clicking the button and giving the particulars in the entry fields „name", „position", „months employed", and/or the combo-boxes „salary group" and „cost center". The user could, for instance, select the cost center *11 subject librarians* and the salary group „A 13" and then click the [filter data records according to the filter criteria] button (cf. *figure 15*). Only those employee data records would then be displayed that fulfill both of those criteria. After clicking the [cancel filtering data records] button (cf. *figure 15*), all of the employee data records are displayed again, thus also those that do not correspond to the filter criteria.

The creation of a staff cost type „assistants" is to be done in the following way: Assistants are *not* recorded by name, and hence also no passwords can be entered. Nevertheless, salary groups for assistants can be set up and selected, e.g. the group SA for student assistants. For this group, the annual costs are to be stated in the pay scale that emerge in a whole year when an assistant performs one working hour per week. After the selection of the salary group, the cost center is to be selected in the corresponding combo-box. The number of working hours (e.g. 55 weekly hours) performed in the cost center by assistants of selected salary group (e.g. SA) is to be entered in the entry field „weekly hours". These values effect the reports according to the following formulas: [The staff costs for assistants of a certain salary group and in a certain cost center = the entry in the entry field „weekly hours" for that cost center x cost value for that salary group] and [The staff capacity of a certain cost center expressed in hours = the entry in the entry field „weekly hours" for that cost center x the constant „work weeks per year for assistants"]. A context tool bar is not shown.

The second tab for the staff cost types is called *entering in data sheet form.* The tab contains two data sheets. One data sheet shows either the entire employee data records or the ones passing the filter. The data records can be modified with the help of the data sheet, e.g. by marking the data record to be altered with a mouse click and then assigning another salary group to it from the data sheet column „salary group". By clicking a column heading, the data records are sorted alphabetically or by ascending value. After another click, the sorting order is changed to a descending one. A second data sheet shows the allocation of the employee selected in the first data sheet in regard to the hours in the cost centers. The allocation can be entered and modified by entries in the data sheet column „annual hours". By means of the F5 function key or by clicking the column heading „annual hours", the annual hours not yet allocated are assigned to a cost center. A data sheet can be printed out by activating it by mouse click and subsequently clicking the corresponding button on the standard tool bar (cf. *figure 15*). Therefore, it is possible, for example, to print out a list of employees without changing into the report mode as is describe further down.

A cost type of the category „formula" allows the formula-related and thereby automated determination of the level of costs for each cost center. It is calculated as follows: [The cost type = constant x the allocation key x the sum of the allocated cost types]. Let us assume that the user selected the node „110 staff costs, civil servants" on the explorer tree and created a new cost type „114 fringe benefits, civil servants" of the type „formula" beneath it. A entry mask belonging to this cost type allows a formula definition with the aid of three tabs.

The tab *cost type formula* contains two combo-boxes. With them, a constant and an allocation key can be selected. If the user selects the list entry „none", then a value of „1" is inserted in the formula for the constant and/or for the allocation key. LIBRARYMANAGER offers a large number of automatically calculated allocation keys. The following predefined allocation keys and base values can be selected from the allocation key combo-box:

- „staff ratio" (= the sum of the annual manhours, of a cost center's employees - in other words, civil servants, salaried employees, workers, and assistants - in relationship to the total manhours performed.

- „amount of civil servant employees per cost center" (= the number of the civil servants allocated to the cost center),

- „amount of civil servant positions per cost center",

- „share of civil servants" (= number of civil servant positions in relationship to the total number of civil servant positions in the library,

- „amount of salaried employees per cost center",

- „amount of salaried positions per cost center",

- „share of salaried employees",

- „amount of working employees per cost center",

- „amount of working positions per cost center",

- „share of workers",

- „PC-ratio", as well as

- „capital commitment".

The calculation of the two allocation keys mentioned last are explained further down in connection with the operating resource cost types. The calculation of the cost type „114 fringe benefits, civil servants" for each individual cost center is an example for the use of a cost type of the category „formula" One has to create a constant „benefit amount" and select it in the entry mask. In addition, the entry „amount of civil servant employees per cost center" is to be selected in the combo-box with the heading „x allocation key". LIBRARYMANAGER then automates the calculation of the cost level needed for every cost center and takes the intervenient data changes into account in the calculation, let us say a modified benefit amount. Allocation keys such as the „square meter ratio" of a cost center are to be defined by the user himself. To do that, the [create new allocation keys] button on the context tool bar (cf. *figure 15*) is to be clicked. In the dialog that then follows, the name for the new allocation key can be entered. By using the corresponding buttons on the context tool bar, the name of the user-defined allocation keys can be modified or deleted (cf. *figure 15*).

The tab *x sum cost types* serves the purpose of taking the sum of other cost types, ascertained for an individual cost center into consideration in the formula. For instance, you would need to create a constant „rate for calculatory retirement pay" for the cost type „113 calculatory retirement pay" and select it in the combo-box. The cost types „111 staff costs, civil servant, academics" and „112 staff costs, civil servant, non-academics" are then to be assigned with the tab „x sum cost types". Assuming that the constant has a value of 0.30 and that the above mentioned cost type in the cost center *11 subject librarians* has a value of 1 Million EUR, then the operation sheet shows an amount of 300,000 EUR for the formula cost type „113 calculatory retirement pay" for this cost center. The cost type „180 administrative overheads surcharge" also belongs to the formula category. The formula consists of a constant that is to be multiplied with a sum of several staff cost types.

Two list fields allow the inclusion of cost types in a formula. The left list field contains the cost types not included, the right list field the cost types included. The assignment of a cost type requires it to be marked by a mouse click in the left field, followed by a subsequent click on the [right arrow] button. The cost type then moves out of the left list field into the right list field and is assigned to the formula. If an assignment needs to be cancelled, then the corresponding cost type is to be selected out of the right list field and moved to the left list field by clicking the [right arrow] button. Only cost types can be assigned that have been placed in the cost type accounting hierarchically above the formula cost type considered and that are not of the type „structure".

The tab with the heading *allocation key* can only be activated by mouse click when a user-defined allocation key (for example „square meter ratio") has been chosen in the allocation key combo-box. The data sheet shows all cost centers and allows the allocation key definition in the column with the heading „quant. share / %". In principle, two procedures are possible when setting each given cost center proportion of the allocation key. On the one hand, the so-called „base values for allocation keys" for each given cost center can be determined, on the other hand, the cost center's percentage proportion of the allocation key. This is illustrated by the example of the allocation key „square meter ratio". Let us assume that the cost center *11 subject librarians* has a floor space of 250 square meters in relation to a total library floor space of 17,500 square meters. The user can then set the allocation key by recording the base value in the corresponding data sheet column. In other words, the user can mark the data sheet line „11 subject librarians" with a mouse click and then enter 250 into the column „quant. share / %". The other possibility lies in entering the percentage proportion, in other words the result of (250/17,500) x 100 = 1.43. The only difference is in the definition and interpretation (units of quantity, or % proportion, respectively) of the values to be entered. In regards to cost accounting, LIBRARYMANAGER treats both variants the same, due to the fact that a cost center's allocation key proportion is calculated as the relationship of the allocation key value for that cost center to the sum of all allocation key values. However, for the purpose of a higher transparency, the determination using the base values for allocation keys is to be preferred over using the percentage proportions.

Furthermore, cost types of the types „single values, direct", „single values, prorated", and „single values, direct and prorated" can be created. The cost type of the type „single values, direct" on the explorer tree has an entry mask that is made up of two tabs, whereby the tab *unit value* is self-explanatory. The tab *direct costs* is for the most part identically structured to the allocation key tab. Both tabs are only different in that here the data sheet column „quant. share / %" is replaced by a column with the heading „direct costs". In this column, the costs belonging to this cost type from the cost center selected in the data sheet can be gathered. Let us assume that the cost type „211 scientific literature: monographs" is of this type. The media costs, for instance for the cost center *33.2 textbook collection use area*, can then be entered in the data sheet column „direct costs".

The selection of a cost type „single values, prorated" leads to the display of an entry mask made up of two tabs. The tab *single value* allows, by means of an entry field, the calculation of a cost amount that is allocated to the cost centers on the basis of an allocation key. The allocation key can be selected on this tab with the help of a combo-box. For the ascertainment of the cost amount, the calculator explained in the section „defining a cost model" is available upon the activation of the entry field. The procedure of defining and selecting an allocation key was described above in the section on the cost types of the category „formula". An example for a cost type of this category is the cost type „312 postage costs". An allocation key „postage costs proportion" could be defined and allocated to the cost type. With the help of this postage costs proportion, the costs are allocated to the cost centers.

Cost types of the type „single values, direct + prorated" represents a mixed form. The three tabs of the entry masks are identical to the tabs of the two categories „single values" in regards of their set-up. For instance, the user is allowed to record the costs for this cost type with the help of an entry field on the tab „single value", or to create an allocation key, select it in a combo-box, and process it with the tab *allocation key*. In addition, costs can be allocated to individual cost centers beforehand using the tab *direct costs*. To do that, the cost center costs are to be recorded in the data sheet column „direct costs". These cost center costs represent a partial amount of the total amount assessed for this cost type on the tab „single value". LIBRARYMANAGER prevents the entry of direct cost center costs above the total amount A cost center to which costs were directly assigned is prorated no further costs of this cost type when ascertaining the operation sheet. The total amount assessed is first diminished by the direct cost center costs and the residual amount is then allocated in a second step to those cost centers that no direct costs have been assigned to. In this respect, the allocation key for a cost type of this category is recalculated while disregarding the allocation key values for cost centers that direct cost have been assigned to.

An example will show the usage possibilities of this cost type. Let us assume that the cost type „313 long distance data transfer costs" is of the category „single values, direct + prorated". This category is user defined since the bulk of the costs of this cost type can be exactly allocated to certain cost centers on the basis of invoices and statistical records. For lack of information, however, a residual amount cannot be directly assigned to cost centers. It will now be allocated with the aid of the allocation key „PC ratio" to those cost centers that the costs are not directly assigned to. The creation of a cost type of the category „single values, direct and prorated" is always advantageous when partial amounts of this cost type can be precisely allocated to individual cost centers and, for simplification reasons, a residual amount is to be prorated to the other cost centers.

For the assessment of depreciations, two categories of cost types are available: „operating resources, direct" and „operating resources, prorated". The entry of an operating resource is done identically for both categories of cost types. The only difference is in how the operating resources is allocated to the cost centers making use of it. There are text box controls on the tab *operating resource* for the specification of the operating resources. In order to create a new data record for operating resources, the corresponding button on the context tool bar needs to be clicked. Furthermore, this tool bar contains buttons for navigating as well as for filtering and deleting those data records (cf.

figure 15). After the creation of a new data record for an operating resource, the name (e.g. laser scanner), the year of acquisition (e.g. 1997), the planned useful life (e.g. 4 years), the number (e.g. 2 pieces), as well as the expenditure per piece (e.g. 5,000 DM) is to be entered into the corresponding entry fields. In addition, the check box „acquisition in second half of the year" can be activated. In this case, only a half of the annual depreciation for the operating resource is shown in the year of acquisition and in the accounting period of the last depreciation offsetting. LIBRARYMANAGER uses the straight-line depreciation method.

Data records for operating resources are often to be entered with only a few changes (e.g. different periods of acquisition). It then makes sense to first enter an operating resource and then make it a „sample" by clicking the corresponding check box. If a further operating resource with identical primary data is to be recorded, click the [create new operating resource] button on the context tool bar and then click the [...] button next to the entry field for the name of the operating resource. In a dialog, all of the operating resources defined as a sample will be displayed on a list field and can be selected by mouse click. The primary data can be transferred to the newly created operating resource by clicking the [OK] button. In the dialog for the selection of an operating resource sample, there is, furthermore, an [cancel] button, which interrupts the data transfer to the newly created operating resource, as well as a [delete] button, which serves the purpose of deleting the element marked in the list of operating resource samples. The cancellation of the sample characteristic does not mean that the operating resource itself is also deleted out of the database. The entries can alternatively be carried out in the tab *record in data sheet form*.

The cost type category „operating resource, direct" provides for the direct assignment of an operating resource to one or more cost centers. To do that, those cost centers using the operating resource are to be selected one after another from the combo-box on the tab *operating resources*, and a value is to be entered in the entry field „quant. share / %".There are two alternative allocation variations. The first one consist of recording the value or respectively a partial value of the piece number of the operating resources entered in the entry field „number". Let us assume that three laser scanners were recorded in the entry field „number". One could then, for example, select the cost center *31 local loans* and assign 2 pieces there and afterwards 1 piece to the cost center *52 computing services*. The other alternative is to do a percentage allocation of the operating resource in this entry field. If, for instance, a copier is used in a 70/30 relationship by the cost centers *51 administration* and *31 local loans*, then the cost centers are to be selected one after another, and a 70, or a 30, respectively, is to be entered into the entry field „quant. share / %". The allocation of operating resources to the cost centers can again be done with the aid of the tab „record in data sheet form" This data sheet contains a column „quant. share / %" for the allocation. The operating resource to be assigned is to be marked beforehand by mouse click on the first data sheet. The data records of this data sheet can be sorted alphabetically or by ascending value by clicking one of the column's headings. After clicking it again, the sorting order is changed to a descending one. By clicking the [print data sheet] button on the standard tool bar (cf. *figure 15*), the list of operating resources can be printed out.

To filter the operating data records resource the corresponding button on the context tool bar needs to be clicked (cf. *figure 15*). Entries can be made in the fields „name" and „acquisition year" and/or a cost center can be selected. In addition, all of the operating resources belonging to the cost type considered which have already been completely depreciated can be identified with the aid of a check box with the label „already depreciated". These operating resource data records could be deleted from the database. In doing so, attention needs to be paid to avoid deleting a PC if it has indeed already been depreciated completely, but is still in use. It is still needed in the automatic calculation of the *PC-ratio*. This option is especially useful for the database maintenance during the continuance of the cost accounting.

An example for a cost type of the category „operational resources, prorated" is the cost type „510 depreciations building/building technology". In this cost type the depreciations are prorated against the cost centers by means of the square meter ratio. The allocation key is to be defined analogously to the procedure explained in the section about cost types of the category „formula". It is then to be selected in the combo-box of the tab *operating resources.*

Cost types of the category „operational resources, direct" and „operational resources, prorated" are the basis for the automated calculation of a cost center's capital commitment and PC-ratio. Only if an operational resources name of begins with the letters „PC", it is entered into the calculation of the PC-ratio. For the calculation of the average fixed capital in a cost center, the software divides the sum of the purchase expenditures of all of the operational resources assigned to this cost center by the factor „2". The calculated value represents the reference base for the ascertainment of the calculatory interest assigned to this cost center. A constant „adequate target rate" (e.g. 0.06) and a cost type of the category „formula" are to be created. The constant and the capital commitment are to be allocated to the formula with the aid of corresponding combo-boxes. LIBRARYMANAGER then calculates the calculatory interest for every cost center for the average capital commitment. The following will now show how cost centers and sub-processes are to be integrated in the cost model.

Cost Centers and Sub-Processes

When marking the node *cost centers* on the explorer tree, a entry form with a tab of the same name then opens. This tab contains a data sheet for processing the number, name, and documentation of the cost centers already entered. The [create a new cost center] button (cf. *figure 15*) is selectable on the standard tool bar. When clicking the arrow next to the button, the options „structure" and „cost centers" can be chosen from the context menu. When clicking the button itself, these options can be chosen from in a dialog. The option „structure" is for the hierarchization of the cost center accounting (e.g. for the computation of totals in reports) LIBRARYMANAGER supports the creation of up to five cost center hierarchical levels. For instance, one can insert and subsequently mark a node of the type „structure" under the node „cost centers" in the explorer tree. A new cost center can only be inserted when the node „cost centers" or a node of the category „structure" has been marked on the explorer tree. When selecting a cost center node, an entry mask with at least one tab then appears in the data entry area of the working area. This tab is called *cost center* and contains entry fields for the entry of a cost center's number (e.g. 10), name (e.g. acquisition), and documentation. In order to attach a node *11 subject librarian* on the explorer tree below the node *10 acquisition* you need to

- mark *10 acquisition*,
- click the [create a new cost center] button, and
- select the „cost center" option.

Afterwards, the newly inserted node is to be marked and the number and name of the cost center are to be entered.

When a node is marked that was generated with the option „cost center" instead of „structure", the tabs *allocation key* and *sub-processes* are made visible in the entry mask in addition to the tab *cost center*. The tab *allocation key* consists of a data sheet with the columns „name", „quant. share / %", and „sum / %". This data sheet has the purpose of listing all of the user-defined allocation keys together with their attributes for the cost center marked. The column „sum / %" is for giving information about the sum of the allocation key values entered for all cost centers. Exclusively the allocation key values assessed for the marked cost centers can be processed in the column „quant. share / %". The other two column are blocked against entries. The context tool bar talked about further above in connection with cost types of the category formula is available for creating new allocation keys and for deleting existing ones, as well as for changing the allocation key name. The changing of the name and the deletion require the allocation key to be selected on the data sheet beforehand.

The tab *sub-processes* uses a data sheet for displaying those sub-processes that have already been assigned to the cost center. In the corresponding data sheet column, the sub-process number, its name, and the percentage proportion of the cost center staff capacity allocated to a sub-process can be altered. The status bar shows how many percent of the cost center's staff capacity has already been allocated and how many percent are still to be allocated.

When a cost center node or a sub-process node belonging to the cost center is marked on the explorer tree, a *new* sub-process can be generated by using the process button on the standard tool bar (cf. *figure 15*). It will be attached to the cost center as a subordinate node on the explorer tree. Following the selection of the new sub-process, an entry mask with two tabs opens (cf. *figure 14*). The tab sub-process contains

- an entry field for the sub-process documentation,
- a group control, which includes the entry fields „number (e.g. 11.1), „name" (e.g. selecting media to order), and „staff capacity in percentage terms" (e.g. 11.42), as well as
- the options fields „dependent on the activity quantity" and „independent of the activity quantity".

A dial field that increases or decreases the percentage proportion in 1% intervals simplifies the assessment of the staff capacity. For the mathematical ascertainment and simultaneous recording of the capacity proportion, a calculator is available in the entry field „staff capacity". If the option „ dependent on the activity quantity „ has been activated, a *cost driver* can be allocated to the sub-process using a combo-box. The context tool bar contains buttons that allows

- a new cost driver to be created,
- the data of cost driver to be modified, or
- a cost driver to be deleted (cf. *figure 15*).

The cost driver's number (e.g. MG 015) and name (e.g. the number of media acquired) are to be entered or modified in a dialog. Furthermore, the cost drivers amount is to be specified in this dialog. Two entry fields are available for this: one of them for the entry of the annual *actual* amount (e.g. 4,000), and the other one for the entry of the cost drivers amount achievable under normal conditions („normal amount"), in other words, the *normal capacity* (e.g. 5,000). Activity expense ratios and activity processing time are always ascertained in relationship to the normal capacity. If the normal capacity has not been determined, then they are shown in relationship to the actual amount. In this case, the value entered in the field „actual amount" is automatically applied to the field „normal amount". On the basis of the relationship of the actual amount to the normal capacity, LIBRARYMANAGER ascertains the used-capacity costs of sub-processes and shows them in the reports. The used-capacity costs are calculated as the product of sub-process costs and the relationship of the actual capacity to the normal capacity. The remaining sub-process costs represent the sub-process's idle-capacity costs. The used time and idle time can be shown analogously.

The tab *direct costs* contains a data sheet, with the help of which the cost center costs of a certain cost type can be completely allocated to a sub-process in that cost center. Only those cost types can be assigned that are not of the category „structure". The check box for the cost type is to be activated in the data sheet column „direct costs". Only the cost center total costs minus the costs assigned to the sub-processes beforehand are then allocated according to the sub-processes' proportion of the cost center staff capacity.

Software Supported Time Logging
In the following, an alternative to the manual assessment of sub-process proportions of the cost center staff capacity will be described: LIBRARYMANAGER's *time logging module*. The objective of the time logging module is to support sub-process-related working time logging by the employee and to automate the evaluation of the time logging data. In order to employ the module, the cost center structure, the sub-process structure, and the staff related cost types have to have been set up. Furthermore the allocation of the employees to the cost centers has to have been done. These data are then to be exported to an independent database. To do that, the node „module" and the tab *time logging* in the entry mask are to be selected. Subsequently, the [export data] button on the context tool bar (cf. *figure 15*) is to be clicked. The path name and a file name for the database to be exported are to be given in a dialog. LIBRARYMANAGER automatically adds the extension „".AUF" to the file name. This file is then to be made available to those employees who are involved in the time logging. It is to be recommended to save the file on a network drive that the employees have access to with their client computers. An alternative to that would be to save the file locally on the computers at the work place.

The next step is to install LIBRARYMANAGER's time logging module on the employees' PCs according to the installation routine described at the beginning of the chapter. When the employees click on the time logging module's program icon, a working screen appears like the one shown in *figure 16*.

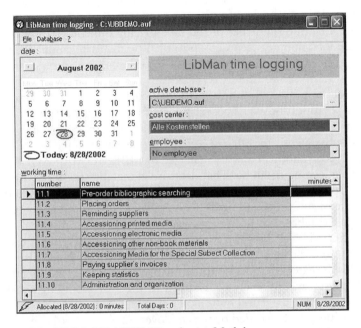

Fig. 16: LIBRARYMANAGER Time logging Module

At first, the employees need to open the database exported from LIBRARYMANAGER. The „open file..." command in the file menu serves that purpose. Alternatively, the [...] button next to the entry field „active database" (cf. *figure 16*) can be used. Please keep in mind, that the last file opened in a program session is automatically opened again the next time the time logging module program is started. Subsequently, the employee has to select the cost center that he works in and his name with the help of the combo-box shown in *figure 16*. This procedure is to be repeated as needed if the employee works in different cost centers. In certain cases after the selection of his name, the employee has to enter his password chosen in LIBRARYMANAGER. Other employees are thereby prevented, particularly when the database is saved on a network drive, from looking at the working time to be gathered daily for the sub-processes. The time logging module represents the sub-processes carried out within a cost center in data sheet form. To record the working time, the employee first needs to select the date on the calendar that the time logging is to be done for. By clicking the calendar entry „today", the current date is marked on the calendar. In the data sheet column „minutes", the working time expended on that date for the sub-processes shown can be entered. At the same time, the status bar of the time logging module gives information about the total minutes recorded up to then on that date, about the number of days so far on which the employee has recorded, and the assessment period to date.

In order to regard the employees' time logging data in a cost model as a percentage proportion of the cost center staff capacity, the following steps are necessary: The first thing to do is to click the node „model" on the explorer tree and subsequently the tab *time logging*. The time data entered by the employees are saved in another database managed by LIBRARYMANAGER, the so-called time logging database. That database is thereby still isolated from the cost model and can be imported successively into LIBRARYMANAGER for the update of sub-processes times if a possible need for correction occurs. In case such a database has not yet been assigned to the cost model, a new one is to be created by clicking the corresponding button on a context tool bar; a path name and file name are to be entered. LIBRARYMANAGER automatically adds the extension „.TIM" to the file name. An already existing time logging database can optionally be assigned to the cost model by clicking the [open time logging database] button on a context tool bar (cf. *figure 15*). Afterwards, the time data recorded by the employees, in other words, the files with the extension „.AUF", are to be imported into this time logging database. The [import time logging data] button on the context tool bar (cf. *figure 15*) is to be used for that. A dialog appears that, aside from a few exceptions, corresponds with the construction of the working screen of the time logging module shown in *figure 16*. The path of the „.AUF" file to be imported can be entered by means of the [...] button.

In case of implausibility's (e.g. the working time entered exceeds the maximal working time possible), the sub-process times recorded by the employees can be corrected analogously to the procedure described above before the „.AUF" file is imported. The employee passwords are not asked for here because only the supervisor of the cost model attains access to the employee data after entering his own password. By clicking the [import] button, the data from the „AUF" file are integrated into the time logging database. In case the „AUF database has not been made available on the network drive, but rather the employees have entered their time data into local databases, every local database is to be individually imported in this way. *Figure 17* summarily represents the interface between LIBRARYMANAGER and the time logging module.

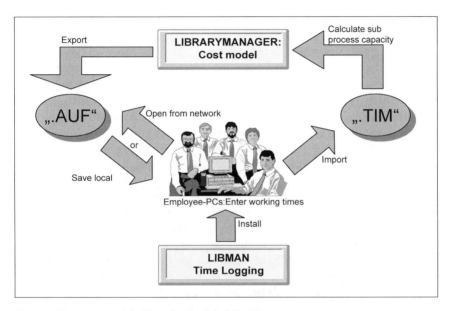

Fig. 17: Integration of the Time logging Module

Furthermore, LIBRARYMANAGER's tab „time logging" provides the possibility of processing, correcting, and deleting time data that have been imported. In this respect, this tab corresponds to the time logging model shown in *figure 16* in regards to set-up and operation. Work minutes on a particular date can be deleted out of the time logging database by selecting an employee's name and a date and then clicking the [delete] button on the context tool bar (cf. *figure 15*). Clicking the [recalculate staff capacity proportions] button on a context tool bar (cf. *figure 15*) effects an update of the cost model. The sub-processes' proportions of the cost centers' staff capacity are recalculated on the basis of the data in the time logging database and taken into account in the cost model. Please keep in mind that the capacity proportions are only updated for the those cost centers for which the working time data have been imported into the time logging database. Capacity proportions already existing are overwritten with the results of the calculation. Cost centers whose employees have not used the time logging model are not affected by the update.

Main Processes and Business Processes

Clicking the node „process levels" on the explorer tree, two identically constructed tabs appear on the screen. They allow to change the numeration, the name, and the documentation of *main processes* and *business processes* already entered. When the node „main processes", „business processes", or an individual main process or business process is marked, the process button on the standard tool bar (cf. *figure 15*) allows the creation of a main process or a business process. When selecting a main process on the explorer tree, an entry mask consisting of three tabs opens up.

The tab *main process* is for the entry of the main process number, name, and documentation. A cost driver can be selected from a combo-box; and the creation, the modification, and deletion of cost drivers is done using the context tool bar as described before. Furthermore, a check box „prorate to other main processes" can be activated. In that case, the main process's costs and capacities are depreciated against those main processes that the check box has not been activated for. This allocation is done according to the staff capacity proportion of the main processes not to be prorated.

The tab *allocate sub-processes* allocates daq-sub-processes to the main process marked on the explorer tree. There are two list fields: In the left area of the tab, the daq-sub-processes not yet 100% assigned to the main processes are listed. In the right area, the sub-processes are listed that have already been assigned to the main process. To make the assignment, mark a sub-process in the left list and then click the button with an arrow pointing to the right. As a result, the sub-process is moved from the left list to the right list, is marked there, and allocated with the percentage proportion not yet allocated. This percentage to be allocated can be reduced by an entry in the entry field „%". The calculator that has been described above is available in this entry field. For daq-sub-processes to which a cost driver has been assigned, the quantity unit to which the main process uses the sub-process, can alternatively be determined proportionately. An entry in the „quant. share" field is automatically calculated into a percentage value, to be precise, by the following formula: (quantity units entered) / (normal capacity).

If no normal amount has been entered separately, the actual amount of the sub-process is used instead of the normal capacity. Since LIBRARYMANAGER saves this percentage figure using two decimal places, insignificant rounding discrepancies can occur when assigning the quantity units. A combo-box allows the filtering of the lists according to cost centers. For instance, the sub-processes to be shown can be limited to those sub-processes belonging to the cost center *11 subject librarians*. The allocation of a sub-process to the main process can be canceled by marking the concerned sub-process on the list of the sub-processes assigned and afterwards clicking the button with the arrow pointing to the left.

Furthermore, a tab is available for the *allocation* of sub-processes to the main processes *in data sheet form*. The data sheet contains all sub-processes that have already been allocated to the main process and all sub-processes that have not yet been 100% allocated to other main processes. These sub-processes can be allocated to the main process by entries in the tabular column „proportion %" or - when dealing with daq-sub-processes - in the column „quantity share". By selecting a sub-process in the data sheet and by clicking the column heading „proportion %" or by pressing the F5 function key, the main process is assigned the %-proportion of the sub-process not yet allocated. An existing allocation can be adjusted on a percentage basis or can be canceled by entering a zero or by pressing the delete button. Moreover, the allocation of sub-processes to main processes can be undertaken by means of drag & drop. To do that, the sub-process to be assigned is to be marked on the explorer tree by a mouse click and, while holding the left mouse button down, to be drug to the considered main process. As a result, the sub-process appears in the list of sub-processes allocated; its assignment proportion can, if need be, be reduced as has been described. The procedure of assigning the main processes to the business processes is identical to the one of assigning the sub-processes to the main processes. Exclusively those main processes that are not to be prorated against other main processes can be allocated to business processes.

Cost Accounting Objects

If the node „other cost accounting objects" has been chosen on the explorer tree, the number (e.g. 10), name (e.g. regional library), and the documentation of cost accounting objects already entered can be modified by means of a data sheet. A new cost accounting object is created by clicking the corresponding button on the standard tool bar (cf. *figure 15*). When highlighting the new cost accounting object on the explorer tree, a entry mask will be displayed, which contains a tab *other cost accounting objects*. With this, the number, name, and documentation of the calculation objects can be entered. Moreover, a cost driver can be assigned by using the combo-box and can be created, modified, and deleted by using the context tool bar. With the aid of four other tabs, the costs and capacities of the cost centers, sub-processes, main processes, and business processes can be allocated in percentage form based on the cost accounting object. The allocation procedure corresponds basically with the procedure described in connection with the allocation of sub-processes to main processes.

If a daq-sub-process is selected from the list of allocated sub-processes, a check box „incl. iaq-costs" can be activated. In that case, the cost accounting object is additionally burdened with the iaq-costs and iaq-capacities of this sub-process. This check box is also available for the allocation of main processes and business processes to the cost accounting object. These tabs additionally displays a further check box „including allocated main process costs". It is only available on the tab *allocate main processes* when a main process has been selected from the list of the allocated main processes that has not been prorated against other main processes. Analogous to the check box „incl. iaq-costs", it thus burdens the cost accounting object with the main process costs and capacities prorated against the main process.

This demonstrated that a kind of „daq-plus-X-rule" applies for the allocation of process costs and capacities to a cost accounting object. At least the daq-costs and capacities are allocated. In addition, iaq-costs and capacities and, in certain cases, prorated main process costs and capacities can be allocated. It is to be pointed out that a plausibility check is not automatically done for *other cost accounting objects* in regards to the allocation of costs and capacity. If, for instance, a cost center and a sub-process in that cost center were allocated at the same time, the cost accounting object would be erroneously burdened with the same costs and capacities twice.

Generating Reports

The presentation of accounting reports requires changing into the *report mode* by clicking the corresponding button on the explorer tool bar (cf. *figure 15*). LIBRARYMANAGER thereupon carries out voluminous calculations like the ascertainment of the operation sheet and sub-process costs. These calculations can take up to 30 seconds, and even longer when very large amounts of data are dealt with. While calculating, a progress indicator gives information about the current status of the calculation. The cost model calculated beforehand to display the reports is stored then into a new, temporary database in the „Temp" sub-directory of LIBRARYMANAGER's installation path. All of the files located in this sub-directory are deleted at the end of the LIBRARYMANAGER session. For that reason, the user is not allowed to use that directory as a path name for files. Sufficient hard drive capacity available, approximately 2 MB for every cost model opened in the report mode, should be provided for the saving of temporary files on the drive where LIBRARY-

MANAGER has been installed. As a result of this preliminary calculation, the reports can subsequently be generated very much faster.

When changing out of the report mode into the data entry mode and then back into the report mode, the user is asked whether the reports should be based on the cost model's temporary database, or whether the temporary database should be generated anew. In case intervenient data relevant to the reports have been entered or modified, the temporary database is to be generated anew. The duplication of the cost model's database calculated beforehand in the „Temp" directory increases the display speed especially when reports from different cost models are to be comparatively displayed alternately one after the other. To do that, another cost model is to be selected in the report mode in the combo-box of the standard tool bar. A certain report is displayed in LIBRARYMANAGER's report mode when selecting the report's matching node on the explorer tree. It is recommended to take the explorer out of its mooring on the left margin of LIBRARYMANAGER's working screen, in order to make more room for the display of the reports on the monitor.

The [report only budget affective costs] button on the explorer tool bar (cf. *figure 15*) needs to be explained: When the button is activated by mouse click, the accounting report only takes those cost types into account that have been marked as budget affecting (cf. „defining cost types" section). The criteria „budget affective" serves the purpose of taking certain cost types into account or suppressing them in the reports for various analysis objectives. The analysis is thereby limited to those cost types that could be direct influenced by the library's management. When extensive financial autonomy is a given, the staff costs, for instance, also belong to this group.

The LIBRARYMANAGER's report mode offers over 70 reports about cost and capacity, which differentially process the gathered data. The reports are issued in data sheet form as well as additionally as a diagram in numerous cases. Belonging to the most important reports are: Reports about the cost type accounting, operation sheets, staff reports, operating resources reports, reports about the time logging results, about sub-processes, main processes, and business processes, about the process hierarchy, and about cost accounting objects. Besides accounting reports, capacity reports exist, which, for example, make evident the cost center capacity used by a sub-process.

The node „incompletely allocated" is found under the explorer node „cost centers" in the report mode under the node „staff". When selecting this node, LIBRARYMANAGER displays all of the employee capacities not yet completely allocated to the cost centers, including their manhours still to be allocated. This report thereby supports the allocation of employees to the cost centers described in the section „cost types". It is recommended to print out this report especially after a change in the constant value „net working time in hours per year" and in the thereby automatically caused change of the hour related allocation to the cost centers carried out for all employees.

In the report mode, buttons on a context tool bar allow the display of the first, last, previous, and next report pages and the export of the reports (cf. *figure 15*). The navigation to a certain report page is possibly by using the combo-boxes on the context tool bar. Zooming, printing, and setting up of a page can be carried out analogously to common word processing software procedures.

After clicking the [export] button, a dialog appears, in which the export format (e.g. „Excel" or „Word") and the export destination (e.g. „application" or „disk file") can be selected from the combo-boxes. „Application" loads the report directly into, e.g. Word, whereas „disk file" saves the report to a path name that is to be stipulated.

Other LIBRARYMANAGER Functions

Several special LIBRARYMANAGER functions are to be explained next. It is possible to *re-sort* the nodes highlighted on the explorer tree (e.g. the subprocess nodes) with the help of the corresponding arrow buttons on the standard tool bar. The [sorting mode on/off] button (cf. *figure 15*) has to have been activated beforehand. Re-sorting is alternatively possible in the overview data sheets (e.g. cost type data sheet, cost center data sheet) by means of drag & drop by dragging a data sheet line to another line while holding down the left mouse button. Mere assignment, for example, of one cost type to a structural cost type, of one cost center to another structural cost center, or of one subprocess to another cost center can be carried out by drag & drop.

Several cost types can be *increased on a percentage basis* by a certain increment factor by clicking the [percental cost type increase] button on the standard tool bar (cf. *figure 15*) and entering of a percentage value. This function is particularly important for the continuance of the cost accounting, e.g. for taking a price index into account.

A command for the *database compression* is located in the data menu's submenu „database". It serves the purpose of minimizing the cost model's database's size and should be carried out in larger intervals. In case a cost model's database has become damaged, e.g. as a result of a system crash, the user can initiate a repair with the „repair database" command.

Furthermore, the data menu contains a „*currency conversion*" command. A currency conversion can be set by dialog, with which the cost model's original data are converted into another currency (e.g. from $ into €).

With the aid of the [help] button on the standard tool bar (cf. *figure 15*), a help text complimented with numerous screenshots can be displayed, which deepen this chapter's elaborations. LIBRARYMANAGER's help system is made up of two help windows. One window is reserved for the exemplary display of the explorer tree, the other window for the representation and explanation of the entry masks appearing in the data entry area. By clicking one of the nodes on the explorer tree in one help window, those entry masks that LIBRARYMANAGER would show in this context are explained in the other help window.

It is necessary for the continuance of the cost accounting and for the data maintenance in the following years to save the cost model file from the previous year under a new name. The command „save as ..." in the file menu or also Windows explorer can be used to do that. After the subsequent opening of the new file, its data (changes in the sub-process structure, higher or lower values of certain cost types, etc.) are to be updated for the new accounting period.

7 Final Observation: Before You Start ...

This handbook describes the work steps necessary for the construction of a decision-oriented library cost accounting. If you have made the decision to introduce the presented accounting system after having read the literature and having given the software a trial run, there are several points you should have in mind before you start. Although these points do not have anything to do with the economic details of the accounting model, taking them into consideration can nevertheless help you to avoid false expectations and unfounded reservations that are possibly connected with the implementation of the cost accounting.

For instance, excessive expectations of the exactness of the cost information are often placed on the accounting model. The user is at first impressed by the computational algorithm being carried out precisely to the tenth decimal place. However, he responds disappointedly when he finds out that the basic data are a result of estimates, formula assignments, and average examinations. It is to be emphasized that the purpose of a cost accounting is not to deliver a hundred percent accurate image of the operational reality. Cost information offers usually accurate values that are adequately accurate for practical purposes - especially for the purposes of reaching and justifying decisions. Regardless of this fact, an improvement of the cost data gained should be continually work on. Moreover, it is often expected or feared, that the results of the cost accounting generates forced action that makes the rethinking of alternative approaches pointless or does not allow for them at all. The information gained from cost data, however, can always only stimulate actions. The interpretation of the information cannot be taken away from the user. Simply said: The statement: „The bibliographic service ties up 9.5 employee years and causes annual costs of 900,000 DM" can both be interpreted as an indication of a high level of quality as well as an impulse for an accelerated construction of electronic delivery services.

Furthermore, there is the danger of an excessive perfectionism, particularly in the implementation phase of the cost accounting. When the number of the supposedly indispensable sub-processes exceeds a thousand, when the time logging is to be carried out over a period of three months in order to prevent an erroneous assessment, and when even insignificant cost driver quantities are validated by random sample analysis, the project is in danger of getting stuck in the initial phase. When then even the first partial results have to be waited for inappropriately long, an impression of an uncontrollable complexity arises, At the worst, this can lead to a discontinuance of the project. Similar difficulties can arise if the process-oriented accounting model is misunderstood as a general reorganization project. Activity analysis and process optimization can suggest measures like

- downsizing the hierarchical structure,

- building of teams,

- job enrichment and job enlargement,

- fundamental reengineering of all working sequences.

The cost accounting itself, however, should not be overloaded with those goals. Initial barriers could be created that quickly make the project appear too troublesome, too tedious, and in certain cases as library-politically too explosive. In fact, especially in the initial phase, the demands on the accounting system should be clearly limited: It is a matter of cost calculation and cost management, and not one of fundamentally rethinking the organizational framework of the service production.

The question about the „costs of the cost accounting" is often asked. As mentioned before, around a half of an employee year is necessary for the construction of the accounting model. This is a staff requirement that usually can be provided by own contribution. When merely limited to the data update, the continuance phase requires one employee month annually at the most. Process optimization and capacity management, on the other hand, represent continual tasks for the library management. Since they totally depend on the on site conditions, no concrete time requirement can be mentioned for these. Taking into account resource gains obtainable by thorough cost management, this deployment will pay off in any case. Moreover, it should also be kept in mind that quite a few private as well as large public institutions consider it necessary to have an independent „controlling" staff department. If the library is really willing to carry out the cost accounting there will be time for it.

Last but not least, it is to be emphasized once more that the cost accounting does not represent a ridged and closed system that merely has to be worked through. The process-oriented accounting model especially suited for service companies is an open instrument that can and has to be adapted by the user to the calculatory and managerial objectives. It is thus only possible to learn this concept by applying it. Therefore, this handbook is not to be understood as tutorial for construction, but rather as help and stimulus for one's own work. In that sense: Simply begin. We wish you the best success!

Appendix

List of Sub-Processes for the University and Regional Library of Münster

COST CENTER GROUP 10: ACQUISITION

COST CENTER 11: Subject Librarians
1.   Selecting the media to order
2.   Processing media sent on approval
3.   Subject indexing legal deposit monographs
4.   Subject indexing electronic media
5.   Subject indexing purchased media
6.   Holding user instruction courses / carrying out guided tours
7.   Providing subject information via Internet
8.   Advising users
9.   Coordinating collection development in the library system
10. Heading a department
11. Special tasks related to the department
12. Public relations work
13. Project tasks

COST CENTER 12: Acquisitions Department 1: Monographs, Electronic Media, etc.
1.   Pre-order bibliographic searching
2.   Placing orders
3.   Reminding suppliers
4.   Accessioning printed media
5.   Accessioning electronic media
6.   Accessioning other non-book materials
7.   Accessioning Media for the Special Subject Collection Netherlands
8.   Paying supplier's invoices
9.   Keeping statistics
10. Administration and organization
11. Processing media sent on approval
12. Distributing post
13. Coordination with faculties / institutes

COST CENTER 13: Acquisitions Department 2: Periodicals
1.   Placing orders
2.   Searching for, requesting, and reminding legal deposit periodicals
3.   Reminding suppliers
4.   Accessioning periodicals (printed media)
5.   Accessioning periodicals for the Special Subject Collection Nether-
     lands
6.   Distributing periodicals to the sites for usage
7.   Processing invoices
8.   Preparing periodicals for binding
9.   Processing subscription cancellations
10. Advising users
11. Keeping statistics
12. Administration and organization
13. Providing articles from periodicals for inter-library loan.
14. Providing articles for courier service / institutes
15. Accessioning microforms

COST CENTER 14: Newspaper Unit
1.   Preparing Newspapers for Binding (gathering, sorting, taking the
     covers off, checking for completeness, etc.)
2.   Registering current microfilms / microfiches
3.   Registering microfilms / microfiches retrospectively
4.   Claiming missing newspapers
5.   Keeping shelf lists
6.   Processing invoices for payment

COST CENTER 15: Integrated Processing of Legal Deposit Media
1.   Searching for legal deposit media
2.   Requesting of legal deposit media and reminding
3.   Accessioning legal deposit media
4.   Cataloging legal deposit media
5.   Keeping statistics
6.   Administration and organization

COST CENTER 16: Gift and Exchange Unit
1.   Requesting gift and exchange media
2.   Pre-order bibliographic searching of gift and exchange media

3.   Forwarding selected gift and exchange media to subject librarians for decision
4.   Accessioning gift and exchange media
5.   Keeping statistics
6.   Administration and organization

COST CENTER 17: University Publications Unit
1.   Preparing dissertations from Münster University to send to exchange partners
2.   Processing requests for exchange of dissertations
3.   Sorting incoming dissertations
4.   Keeping a list of series titles
5.   Cataloging the dissertations
6.   Final processing
7.   Exchanging university calendars
8.   Keeping statistics

COST CENTER GROUP 20: CATALOGING

COST CENTER 21: Alphabetical Catalog
1.   Cataloging individual works
2.   Cataloging individual works
3.   Cataloging of individual works completely new
4.   Cataloging multivolume works by using a subrecord
5.   Cataloging multivolume works by creating a new subrecord
6.   Cataloging media for the Special Subject Collection Netherlands
7.   Cataloging electronic media
8.   Cataloging other special forms
9.   Controlling catalog entries made
10. Maintaining database of library catalog
11. Processing mailbox communication
12. Supporting retrospective cataloging
13. Administration and organization

COST CENTER 22: Retrospective Cataloging
1.   Cataloging individual works by using MAB-data
2.   Cataloging individual works by using HBZ-data
3.   Cataloging of individual works completely new
4.   Cataloging multivolume works by using a subrecord

5. Cataloging multivolume works by creating a new subrecord
6. Controlling catalog entries made
7. Processing mailbox communication/ requests for corrections
8. Filing back catalog cards
9. Controlling shelf numbers (daily lists)
10. Transferring books from reading room
11. Keeping statistics
12. Administration and organization
13. Coordination with faculties / institutes

COST CENTER 23: Editorial Staff for Serial Catalog Münster
1. Cataloging periodicals
2. Adding holdings statements to Union Catalog of Serials
3. Processing corrections and cases to be checked
4. Coordinating serial cataloging with institutes
5. Keeping statistics
6. Administration and organization

COST CENTER 24: Subject catalog
1. Checking and eventually correcting subject librarians' subject indexing: legal deposit media / media of special subject collection Netherlands / other media
2. Recording keyword chains in union catalog: legal deposit media / media of special subject collection Netherlands / other media
3. Adding new keyword records to database: legal deposit media / media of special subject collection Netherlands / other media
4. Administration and organization

COST CENTER GROUP 30: USE

COST CENTER 31: Local Loans
1. Booking loans
2. Booking returns
3. Issuing library cards
4. Controlling loan periods (making out fine notices and return orders, processing cases of loss, initiating procedures of fining, etc.)
5. Settling fee register (for local loans, inter-library loans, and textbook collection.)
6. Settling cost refunds for electronic document delivery service

7.   Processing courier deliveries
8.   Managing files of the loan system (user data and inventory data)
9.   Processing electronic document delivery
10.   Processing searches for misplaced media
11.   Adapting old shelf marks to automated loan system
12.   Administration and organization
13.   Clearing user's questions.

COST CENTER 32: Inter-library Lending
1.   inter-library lending: booking loans
2.   inter-library lending: forwarding loan form
3.   inter-library lending: preparing media for shipping
4.   inter-library lending: booking returns
5.   Borrowing inter-library loan service: determining routing / sending loan forms / processing returns
6.   Borrowing inter-library loan service: booking orders
7.   Borrowing inter-library loan service: processing and booking receipts
8.   Borrowing inter-library loan service: booking returns
9.   Controlling due dates
10.   Processing invoices
11.   Settling postage register (for local loans, inter-library loans, textbook collection)
12.   Keeping statistics
13.   Advising users
14.   Administration and organization

COST CENTER 33.1: Textbook Collection Work Area
1.   Placing orders
2.   Accessioning media
3.   Cataloging
4.   Processing book binder parcels
5.   Processing media technically
6.   Executing the final control
7.   Booking loans
8.   Booking returns
9.   Reshelving media
10.   Weeding and selling discarded media
11.   Managing service counter

12. Clearing center user services
13. Administration and organization

COST CENTER 34.1: Reading Room Work Area
1. Making media with restricted access available for in-house use
2. Completing photocopy / photo requests for media with restricted access
3. Issuing media from reading room stock
4. Preparing media for inter-library loan
5. Maintenance of reading room stock (adding and weeding media, arrangement and stock revision, sorting new publications to folders, processing search cases and repairs, etc)
6. Taking care of catalog room stock
7. Reference service
8. Maintaining catalog of the reading room stock
9. Providing reserve collections for seminars
10. Managing fee register (fees for use of reader printer and photocopy requests, etc.)
11. Selling library publications
12. Managing lockers
13. Keeping statistics
14. Administration and organization

COST CENTER 35.1: Reference Service Work Area
1. Answering reference questions: orally in person and by telephone
2. Answering reference questions: per e-mail
3. Answering reference questions: written
4. Providing library instruction for users
5. Holding user instruction courses for CD-ROM databases and Internet use
6. Supporting bibliographic services
7. Performing bibliographic services
8. Processing complaints for the electronic document delivery service
9. Processing searches for misplaced media
10. Processing purchase suggestions
11. Maintaining the university library's homepage
12. Making up information material
13. Teaching trainees

14. Administration and organization
15. Taking care of physically challenged users

COST CENTER 36: Stacks Work Area
1. Providing media for distribution / document delivery
2. Reshelving media
3. Revising media collection
4. Filing accessions
5. Rearranging media etc.
6. Planning shelf room
7. Advising users
8. Performing user service for newspaper collection

COST CENTER 37: Supervision Services
1. Controlling

COST CENTER GROUP 40: TECHNICAL SERVICES

COST CENTER 41: Material Purchasing and Technical Services
1. Managing material supplies
2. Obtaining offers
3. Placing orders
4. Reminding suppliers
5. Checking delivery and accessioning items
6. Processing the invoice for remittance
7. Organizing service operation and deployment of staff
8. Administration of grounds / buildings / technical equipment
9. Planning and coordinating space utilization
10. Organizing exhibitions and events
11. Budget control
12. Public relations work
13. Project management
14. Keeping statistics
15. Administration and organization

COST CENTER 42: Mail Room
1. Preparing incoming mail for distribution (signing delivery notes, sorting, and unpacking)
2. Distributing incoming mail

3.   Preparing outgoing mail for sending (packing, prepaying postage)
4.   Providing chauffeur service
5.   Keeping address file for inter-library loan.
6.   Stockpiling and disposing packing material
7.   Keeping statistics

COST CENTER 43: Copy Center
1.   Carrying out copy requests for loan circulation
2.   Carrying out copy requests for reading room
3.   Carrying out copy requests for information services
4.   Making copies of media for preservation purposes
5.   Carrying out other copy requests
6.   Keeping statistics

COST CENTER 44: Technical Book Processing
1.   Processing media technically (making and putting up shelf-mark signs, applying ownership stamp, gluing on booking labels, entering booking number into the loan system)
2.   Making media ready to bind (determining the book binder, selecting the cover pattern, sorting out media units, etc.)
3.   Controlling the book binder parcels (including processing of invoice for remittance)
4.   Carrying out repairs on media
5.   Producing case bindings
6.   Training book binders
7.   Keeping statistics

COST CENTER 45: Custodian Services
1.   Rounds for opening, closing, and controlling
2.   Managing store room (receiving, shelving, and issuing materials, and maintaining a file of materials)
3.   Servicing technical equipment
4.   Servicing photocopy machines
5.   Carrying out minor repairs
6.   Supporting work done by companies
7.   Carrying out disposal measures
8.   Controlling the parking places

COST CENTER GROUP 50: CENTRAL SERVICES

COST CENTER 51: General Administration
1.   Management
1.1   Strategic planning
1.2   Planning and developing organizational structures
1.3   Planning and steering business processes
1.4   Preparing decisions and controlling execution
1.5   Creating IT framework
1.6   Planning space utilization
1.7   Devising collection development profile and ensuring stock preservation
1.8   Coordinating library system
1.9   Project management
1.10 Administrational routines
2.   Finances
2.1   Budget planning and control
2.2   Attracting third party funds and special funds
2.3   Implementing results of cost controlling
2.4   Keeping and coordinating budget control list
3.   Staff
3.1   Implementing and controlling staff development plan
3.2   Developing and implementing plans for staffing requirements
3.3   Managing staff affairs
3.4   Human resource management
3.5   Managing position chart
3.6   Processing recruitment and dismissals
3.7   Staff appraisal
3.8   Managing continual professional education
3.9   Advising employees regarding civil service regulations
3.10 Managing student assistants
3.11 Keeping statistics on absence rates
3.12 Taking care of trainees
3.13 Staff council activity
4.   The public
4.1   Coordinating and performing public relations work
4.2   Working up reports, patterns, etc. for university and other decision making boards.
4.3   Planning events and exhibitions

4.4   Performing work for boards and associations
4.5   Preparing and holding lectures
4.6   Writing publications in the field of library science
5.   Support operations
5.1   Performing writing services
5.2   Connecting and transferring telephone conversations
5.3   Distributing post
5.4   Purchasing and stockpiling office material
5.5   Other administrational work (taking care of guests, filing of records, etc.)
5.6   Keeping statistics

COST CENTER 52: Computing Services
1.   Planning and development
1.1   Planning IT structures and frameworks
1.2   Planning needs, facilities, and implementation as well as preparing purchasing.
1.3   Developing products and applications
1.4   Programming
2.   Server: Providing server performance for ...
2.1   Loan system
2.2   Cataloging
2.3   Databases and catalogs
2.4   Internet services
2.5   Document delivery service
3.   Administration
3.1   Maintaining software for system and applications
3.2   System management (access rights, memory resources)
3.3   System documentation
4.   Operating
4.1   Maintenance, repairs, trouble shooting
4.2   Data storage
4.3   Printing jobs
5.   Connectivity
5.1   Managing network (access rights, net addresses, name, service, etc.)
5.2   Optimization of network performance
5.3   Network documentation
6.   Client: providing computers for work place
6.1   Setting up hardware

6.2   Installing software
6.3   Configuring network connection
6.4   Familiarizing users
7.   User service and continuing education
7.1   Users
7.2   Employees
8.   Online searching office
8.1   Online searches
    a)   Carrying out online searches
    b)   Creating and updating database offers and overviews
    c)   Making up the monthly and annual statistics and accounting checks.
8.2   Online databases
    a)   Creating and maintaining the database „internet literature list"
    b)   Creating and maintaining the database „List of departmental libraries at Münster University"
8.3   User Instruction
    a)   User instruction courses for internet and CD-ROM databases
    b)   Preparing and updating user instruction courses

COST CENTER 53: Service Center Cataloging in Departmental Libraries
1.   Checking and correcting catalog entries from departmental libraries
2.   Tending to hardware and software for departmental cataloging
3.   Maintaining the catalog of departmental libraries
4.   Training cataloging staff from departmental libraries
5.   Advising cataloging staff from departmental libraries
6.   Keeping statistics for the Service Center Cataloging in Departmental Libraries
7.   Administration and organization / internal information
8.   Bibliographical preparation for catalog entries from departmental libraries
9.   Making catalog entries for departmental libraries
10.   Checking catalog entries from departmental libraries
11.   Maintaining union catalog Münster
12.   Keeping statistics union catalog Münster
13.   Administration and organization union catalog Münster

COST CENTER GROUP 60: SPECIAL SERVICES

COST CENTER 61.1: Manuscript Department

1. Sorting through and ordering autographic material
2. Accessioning old books / autographs
3. Cataloging old books / autographs
4. Technically processing old books / autographs
5. Making old books / autographs available for use
6. Performing reference service
7. Processing requests for photographic reproduction
8. Cataloguing autographic material
9. Preparing exhibitions (incl. producing a catalog and other presentations of stock)
10. Administration and organization
11. Active use (returning book to magazine and loan site)
12. Manuscript reading room (supervision and information)
13. Special tasks (making microfiche of articles on Westphalia)

COST CENTER 62: Center for Historical Collections in North-Rhine Westphalia

1. Providing expert opinion on historical library collections
2. Transporting stock to University and Regional Library Münster (incl. return transport)
3. Classifying collections / allotting shelf-marks
4. Pre-order bibliographic searching in online catalogs
5. Cataloging: creating new catalog entries
6. Cataloging: making use of catalog entries from external databases / processing existing data
7. Maintaining provenance file
8. Controlling new catalog entries
9. Producing a catalog
10. Administration and organization
11. Keeping statistics
12. Verifying bibliographic data (incl. biographical information)
13. Slide documentation / making photo work

COST CENTER 63: Editorial Staff, Bibliography of North-Rhine Westphalia (NWB)

1. Searching for NWB-relevant publications

2. Pre-order bibliographic searching NWB-relevant publications
3. Checking acquisitions for NWB-relevant publications
4. Cataloging NWB-relevant maps
5. Cataloging NWB-relevant articles from periodicals / contributions to collections
6. Subject indexing of NWB-relevant publications
7. Examining old collections

COST CENTER 64: Preservation
1. Restoring endangered material
2. Conservation of endangered collections
3. Transferring information to other media (digitalizing, microfilming, etc.)
4. Cataloging microfilmed media
5. Carrying out / tending to mass deacidifying measures
6. Preparing newspaper stock for outsourced microfilming (removing the covers, etc.)
7. Allocation of restoration jobs
8. Maintenance measures for leather, half-leather, vellum, and half-vellum bindings
9. Repairs on cardboard covers cloth bindings
10. Dry-cleaning books
11. Imbedding title pages or frontispiece, adding missing places
12. Fastening of turn-ins, renewing book clasps
13. Wet treatment and leaf casting of individual pages
14. Boxing individual pieces
15. Collating

Glossary

Actual Costs: Actual costs are the costs that actually arise for a cost accounting object (i.e. a cost type or a cost unit) during the current or a past accounting period.

Budgeted Costs: Budgeted costs are the cost ascertained for the planned or predicted activities in a future accounting period. They are cost objectives for controlling and steering the future cost occurrence.

Budgeting: This term denotes the assignment of a certain budget volume to an operational unit that can, for the most part, manage its use autonomously. The first step for budgeting is the globalization of the budget appropriation. This means, special-purpose transfers should be replaced be means eligible as cover for staff-, material-, and investment expenditures and reserve assets. In the final stage of this process, the operational units work with a flat-rate budget allowance (input-oriented budgeting). Output-oriented budgeting, on the other hand, which connects the amount of the approved allowance to the definition of the service product of the operational unit differentiated in regards to costs, quality, and quantity.

Business Process: Extensive fields of services and tasks of a company that are dealt with across functional centers and that arise by linking main processes together. For instance, the library's user services could be defined as a business process that is made up of the main processes „electronic document delivery", „reference services", „loan circulation", „loans", etc. Cost information on the aggregate level of the business processes are primarily intended as information for external decision makers and funders.

Capacity: This term denotes the quantitative performance capability of a company or of an operational unit within a segment of time. The capability of the cost center *local loans* to process one million loans represents the capacity of that department. Furthermore, this term frequently also refers to the resources, particularly staff and capital assets, required for a certain activity quantity. This is, for instance, the staff capacity needed for the realization of a certain activity quantity.

Cost Center Accounting: Cost center accounting answers the question „Where do the costs arise?" Its purpose is to assign the costs to the place of the cost emergence. The cost centers can be divided up according to functional or spatial viewpoints or according to areas of responsibility. The division according to functional aspects suggests itself for libraries so that the chart of functional accounts for the most part corresponds with the division of the department or of the organizational unit.

Cost Driver: The cost driver represents a measuring unit for determining the activity performance. It has two function: on the one hand, the degree that the resources are being used by the process is measured by it; on the other hand, the process's output. An example will demonstrate what is meant by a cost driver: The process „ordering media" rendered in the cost center *acquisition by purchase* is always carried out when an order entry exists. Therefore, the receipt of an order triggers off activities connected with the process of ordering media. Executing those activities consumes resources (working time, material, etc.) and thereby causes costs. The measuring units „number of orders" thus represents the cost determinant, i.e. the cost driver, of the process „ordering media". Further examples of cost drivers are: number of reference questions, number of loans, number of database updates. The cost driver is thus the measuring unit for the extent that resources are used by operating procedures. The number of order entries is so to speak the „driving force behind the costs" of the process „ordering media". Every new incoming order triggers the process and causes the costs connected with its execution. The cost driver is at the same time the reference value for the determination of the output: the number of order entries processed defines the activity quantity of the operating procedure. The cost driver thus represents the decisive measurement for the quantification of the processes, both in regards to the level of cost as well as their activity quantity. Occasionally, the term „cost driver" is related exclusively to the main processes, while the term „measuring unit" is used for the determination of the activity of sub-processes.

Cost Type Accounting: Cost type accounting answers the question „Which costs have arisen?" It task is to divide up and present all costs arising in the framework of service performance within a period according to the criterion „type of production factor". The essential cost type groups of the library are: staff costs, media costs, operating costs, administrative costs, and calculatory depreciations.

Cost Unit Accounting: Cost unit accounting answers the question „What did the costs occur for?" It ascertains the costs of the produced services or products. There are two different kinds of cost unit accountings. The unit-of-output costing calculates the cost occurring for a product unit, e.g. the costs of one document delivery, or of one circulation transaction. Cost unit period accounting ascertains the total costs occurring for the considered cost unit within an accounting period, for example the costs for document delivery services during the first quarter of a fiscal year.

Costs: Costs are evaluated in monetary units to measure the resource consumption caused by the service production within an accounting period.

Direct Costing: This term denotes those cost accounting procedures that allocate the parts (each of which are to be defined separately) of a company's total costs to the considered cost accounting object. It depends upon the given accounting purpose which cost proportions are offset against the cost units, and which are kept on lower steps of the accounting system, i.e. on the steps of cost type accounting or of the cost center accounting. An important case of application of direct costing in service companies is the calculation, relevant costs. Relevant costs are resource consumptions that occur with the decision for a certain service offer.

Disbursement / Expenditure: A disbursement spot is understood to be every decrease of cash assets that is represented as a reduction of cash on hand or of demand balances at credit institutions. Expenditures encompass, moreover, all creditary business transactions, the increase of accounts payable and the decrease of accounts receivable.

Economic Efficiency: This term denotes the favorable relationship between the funds employed and the results obtained. The two most advantageous means-end relations are the following: Either a certain pre-determined result is reached with the least possible employment of funds (minimum principle). Or the best possible result is reached with a certain employment of funds (maximum principle). Economic efficiency is thus a measurement of the relationship of a rendered service to the use of resources needed to do it. It thus denotes the efficiency of the service production.

Effectivity: Effectivity is the degree to which a produced performance fulfills the needs of the user / customer („doing the right things").

Efficiency: This term denotes the relationship of a rendered service to the use of resources required to do it („doing the things right"). Efficiency can be expressed as the quotient of the output (e.g. activity quantity) and the input (e.g. employee hours). This term is often use synonymously with economic efficiency.

Final Cost Centers: This term denotes those cost centers of a company that directly render product related and customer / user related services. Examples of final cost centers in the library are local loans, inter-library loans, and reference services. The final cost centers for their part use up intra-company services of indirect cost centers.

Fixed Costs: This term denotes activity-independent costs, that means those cost that remain constant regardless of changes in the activity quantity. Fixed cost arise through the build-up and the maintenance of service potential, especially by the provision of staff, facilities, and space. The operational readiness is independent of whether and to what degree the service is used. The costs are consequently not influenced by changes in the activity quantity. Fixed costs are also called standby costs or capacity costs. They can only be influenced by the build-up or cutback of operational readiness. The extent to which those dispositions are possible essentially depends on the length of the commitment period of the fixed costs. For instance, the library's staff costs represent long-term fixed costs due to far-reaching dismissal notices in the public sector. Fixed costs for service products are also always overhead costs of those products.

Full Absorption Costing: Unlike direct costing, full absorption costing offsets the entire costs of a company against the cost accounting objects considered, usually against the cost units. The unit costs are assigned directly to the cost units, the overhead costs are allocated with the help of clearing ratios and costing rates. In the public sector, the full absorption costing is primarily employed for the calculation of cost covering remunerations and fees, as well as for the ascertainment of production costs for external information needs.

Indirect Cost Centers: This term denotes those cost centers that render services not directly related to the product or the customer / client, but services for other cost centers of the company. Examples for indirect cost centers in the library are the library administration, or the computing services. Those cost centers that render their services directly to the final products or to the end users are called final cost centers.

Main Process: A main process comes into existence by linking sub-processes from one or more cost centers together. Main processes describe the library's services, in other words the library's products. For instance, the main process „electronic document delivery" is made up of the sub-processes „placing orders", „processing complaints", „processing invoices", and „managing document order delivery system".

Marginal Costs: This term denotes those costs that additionally occur with every further unit of output. As a rule, they are identical with the variable costs of the unit of output.

Operating Resources: All facilities that represent the technical prerequisites for service production and are used for a longer period. Examples are buildings, machines, office outfitting and equipment. Operating resources characteristic for libraries are compact shelving units, security systems for books, self booking equipment, mass deacidifying equipment, etc.

Overhead Costs: Overhead costs are characterized by the fact that they occur for several cost accounting objects together. This has the result that they cannot be directly assigned, but rather only with the help of clearing ratios. If no explicit cost accounting object is mentioned, the cost unit overhead costs are talked about, i.e. the overhead costs of the produced service products. Examples are operating costs, and staff costs (in as much as they do not pertain to costs directly allocable to products). Library costs are for the most part overhead costs.

Prime Costs: The entirety of the costs that arise due to the provision of a library service, in regards to a unit of output. It comprises both the costs directly connected with the service production, as well as proportional costs for the general infrastructure of the library.

Process Hierarchy: The vertical segmentation of the operational procedure into business processes, main processes, and sub-processes. Business processes (e.g. „rendering user services") can be divided into main processes (e.g. „delivering documents electronically", „lending media", „online searches"), which for their part can be segmented again into sub-processes (e.g. „processing orders", „processing complaints", „processing invoices"). In principle, this hierarchy can be developed both downward and upward. An example for „downward" would be the application of activities, that sub-processes are made of (e.g. „scanning the document"). The process hierarchy allows the structured non-overlapping representation of the library's operational procedures.

Process depending on the activity quantity: Processes depending on the activity quantity (daq) vary in the number of their executions depending upon the activity quantity in the cost center. Concerning daq-processes, the necessary time required and correspondingly the costs to be assigned are proportional to the volume of work. The latter is expressed by the cost driver of the process. For instance, the employee use needed for the execution of the process „cataloging media" depends directly upon the number of the acquired media.

Process independent of the activity quantity: Processes independent of the activity quantity (iaq) are independent of the activity quantity of a cost center. They occur through the mere existence of the cost center and serve the preparation and support of the processes depending on the activity quantity. An examples of an iaq-processes is „heading the department". Since iaq-processes occur quantity fixed, there is no cost driver to be designated for them.

Process: A process is a chain of activities connected in a logical and chronological way, that is aimed at rendering an output. The process is characterized by a certain resource usage to be evaluated in costs, as well as by a cost determinant (cost driver), that serves as a measuring unit for the number of process executions. To delimit a process from the upstream and downstream activities, it can additionally be described in regards to the starting event triggering it and the concluding event completing it.

Product: This term denotes the performances that a company produces for external customers or users. The library's products are its services, such as, for instance, the delivery of documents, the provision of internet work places, and the lending of media. Services can usually be regarded as main processes, which for their part are described as the linking together of sub-processes. In a broad sense, the term „product" does not only refer to the services produced for the external demander, but also to the internal services that one organizational unit renders for another. In this sense, for instance, the implementation of a new loan system is specified as a product.

Production Factor: Production factors are all of the resources used within the framework of service production (staff, machines, material, energy, etc.). They can be divided into the categories of usage factors and consumption factors. Usage factors are not consumed by the one time use in the service production process, but are available for a multitude of utilizations. Their potential is thus only used up over time. Belonging to the group of usage factors are, for instance, permanently employed staff, as well as capital assets and buildings; in libraries, also the collection. The sizing and combination of usage factors determines the capacity of an operational unit. Consumption factors on the other hand are completely consumed when used a single time in the service process (e.g. materials). In the production of the library services, they only play a minor role. Things like labeling material, shipping envelopes, or user cards are among those.

Relevant Costs: Relevant costs are costs dependent upon decisions. They comprise those resource consumptions that additionally occur as a result of a decision for a certain service offer. Therefore, they are to be taken into account when evaluating that decision in regards to the costs. The relevant costs, for instance, for the decision to join an online delivery consortium are costs of the hardware and software to be purchased as well as staff costs. However, the costs for the network and the PC infrastructure already available, or the operating costs are not relevant costs.

Sub-Process: A sequence of activities in a cost center belonging together logically and chronologically, that can be assigned to one or more main processes. A sub-process is always an operation within one cost center. It thereby represents the connecting link between cost centers and cost-center-overlapping main processes, which for their part are formed by linking sub-processes together. A sub-process in the cost center *local loans* is for example the activity „recording loans".

Unit Costs: Unit costs are those costs that can be directly assigned to a cost accounting object, that means without using clearing ratios. If no explicit cost accounting object is mentioned, those costs that are clearly and directly allocable to the service products are usually talked about. Unit costs of cost units are always variable costs. The unit costs' proportion of the total costs in libraries is - as generally in service companies - insignificantly low, and overhead costs dominate.

Utilization: This term describes the exploitation or the degree of exploitation of the capacity of an operational unit. Say, the online searching office has a capacity of 500 online searches a month, as far as its workforce and outfitting is concerned., However, if only 300 searches are asked for by the user, the utilization degree amounts to 60%.

Variable Costs: Variable costs change automatically with the increase or decrease of the activity quantity. That means, no additional dispositions and decisions are needed. Due to their dependence upon the activity quantity, they are also called output-related costs. An examples of variable costs are the costs for shipping materials and postage occurring for the delivery form „postal dispatch" when dealing with electronic delivery orders. If the term „variable costs" is not characterized any closer, the dependency of the cost amount on the activity quantity is meant. Otherwise, the cost determinant, which in regards to the costs is to be considered as variable, is to be explicitly stated. The same goes for the complementary term „fixed costs". For instance, the costs of a private sentry used for library exhibitions are fixed per exhibition, but variable in regards to the number of exhibitions per accounting period.

Bibliography

Ambrosy, R./Heise, St./Kirchhoff-Kestel, S./Müller-Böling, D. (1997): Integrierte Kostenrechnung: Unterwegs in Richtung zu einem modernen Hochschulmanagement. Ergebnisse des CHE-Projektes 'Kostenrechnung an den Fachhochschulen Bochum und Dortmund' und deren Umsetzung im Bochumer Kostenrechnungsmodell, Wissenschaftsmanagement 3, pp. 204-213.

Backhaus, K./Funke, St. (1997): Fixkostenmanagement, in: Kostenmanagement. Wettbewerbsvorteile durch systematische Kostensteuerung, hrsg. von Franz, K.-P./Kajüter, P., Stuttgart, pp. 29-43.

Becker, R. (1997): Kapazitätsmanagement in der Verwaltung - eine prozeßorientierte Analyse, in: Kapazitätsmanagement in Dienstleistungsunternhmungen. Grundlagen und Gestaltungsmöglichkeiten, hrsg. von H. Corsten und St. Stuhlmann, Wiesbaden, pp. 199-219.

Behrens, T. (1996): Globalisierung der Hochschulhaushalte. Grundlagen, Ziele, Erscheinungsformen und Rahmenbedingungen, Neuwied.

Beinhauer, M./Schellhaas, K.-U. (1997): Gemeinkosten- und Ressourcenmanagement im administrativen Bereich, in: Kostenmanagement. Neuere Konzepte und Anwendungen, hrsg. von C.-C. Freidank, Berlin/Heidelberg, pp. 403-423.

Benkert, W. (1998): Einführung in die Kostenrechnung, in: Wege zu einer bibliotheksgerechten Kosten- und Leistungsrechnung, hrsg. vom Deutschen Bibliotheksinstitut, Berlin, pp. 21-40 (dbi-Materialien 167).

Bertsch, L.H. (1991): Expertensystemgestützte Dienstleistungskostenrechnung, Stuttgart.

Brinckmann, H. (1998): Die neue Freiheit der Universität. Operative Autonomie für Lehre und Forschung an Hochschulen, Berlin (Modernisierung des öffentlichen Sektors 10).

Budäus, D. (1997): Controlling als integratives Element von Verwaltungsreformen, in: Kostenrechnung: Stand und Entwicklungsperspektiven. Wolfgang Männel zum 60. Geburtstag, hrsg. von W. Becker und J. Weber, Wiesbaden, pp. 27-41.

Ceynowa, K. (1997): Prozeßkostenrechnung in Hochschulbibliotheken, Wissenschaftsmanagement 3, pp. 302-309.

Ceynowa, K. (1994): Von der 'Dreigeteilten' zur 'Fraktalen' Bibliothek. Benutzerzentrierte Bibliotheksarbeit im Wandel: das Beispiel der Stadtbibliothek Paderborn. Würzburg.

Ceynowa, K./Finkeißen, A. (1998): Prozeßkostenmanagement für wissenschaftliche Bibliotheken, in: Prozeßkostenmanagement. Methodik und Anwendungsfelder, hrsg. von der Horváth & Partner GmbH, 2. völlig neubearb. Aufl., München, pp. 465-480.

Coenenberg, A.G. (1997): Kostenrechnung und Kostenanalyse, 3. überarb. und erw. Aufl., Landsberg/Lech.

Cooper, R./Kaplan, R.S. (1999): Integrierte Kostensysteme - Verheißung und Gefahr zugleich, Harvard Business Manager 21, pp. 76-86.

Cooper, R./Kaplan, R.S. (1995): Messung der Kosten der Ressourcennutzung durch prozeßorientierte Systeme, in: Prozeßkostenrechnung. Bedeutung, Methoden, Branchenerfahrungen, Softwarelösungen, hrsg. von W. Männel, Wiesbaden, pp. 43-58.

Cooper, R./Kaplan, R.S. (1988): Measure Costs Right: Make the Right Decisions, Harvard Business Review 66, pp. 96-103.

Corsten, S. (1997): Dienstleistungsmanagement, 3. völlig neu bearb. Aufl., München.

DIN Deutsches Institut für Normung e.V. (Hrsg.) (1998): Bau- und Nutzungsplanung von wissenschaftlichen Bibliotheken, 2. Aufl., Berlin/Wien/Zürich.

Eichhorn, P./Bräunig, D. (1997): Kosteninformationen zur Steuerung öffentlicher Verwaltungen, in: Kostenrechnung: Stand und Entwicklungsperspektiven. Wolfgang Männel zum 60. Geburtstag, hrsg. von W. Becker und J. Weber, Wiesbaden, pp. 105-125.

Finkeißen, A. (1997): Softwareunterstützung im Prozeßmanagement, in: Qualitätscontrolling. Ein Leitfaden zur betrieblichen Navigation auf dem Weg zum Total Quality Management, hrsg. von der Horváth & Partner GmbH, Stuttgart, pp. 221-246.

Fischer, T.M. (1997): Neue Wege im Kostenmanagement - Einsatzmöglichkeiten der Prozeßkostenrechnung in öffentlichen Unternehmen, in: Controlling öffentlicher Einrichtungen, hrsg. von H.-G. Baum u.a., Stuttgart, pp. 145-167.

Franz, K.-P./Kajüter, P. (1997): Proaktives Kostenmanagement als Daueraufgabe, in: Kostenmanagement. Wettbewerbsvorteile durch systematische Kostensteuerung, hrsg. von Franz, K.-P./Kajüter, P., Stuttgart, pp. 5-27.

Friedl, B. (1997): Kapazitätsplanung und -steuerung als Bezugsobjekt des Kostenmanagements in Dienstleistungsunternehmungen, in: Kapazitätsmanagement in Dienstleistungsunternehmungen. Grundlagen und Gestaltungsmöglichkeiten, hrsg. von H. Corsten und St. Stuhlmann, Wiesbaden, pp. 111-135.

Funk, R. (1975): Kostenanalyse in wissenschaftlichen Bibliotheken. Eine Modelluntersuchung an der Universitätsbibliothek der Technischen Universität Berlin, Pullach bei München (Bibliothekspraxis 17).

Gaiser, B. (1998): Prozeßkostenrechnung und Activity Based Costing (ABC), in: Prozeßkostenmanagement. Methodik und Anwendungsfelder, hrsg. von der Horváth & Partner GmbH, 2. völlig neubearb. Aufl., München, pp. 65-77.

Griebel, R. (1999): Outsourcing in der Erwerbung - neue Zauberformel oder Weg zu effektivem Beschaffungsmanagement?, in: Nur was sich ändert, bleibt. 88.Deutscher Bibliothekartag in Frankfurt am Main 1998, hrsg. von S. Wefers, Frankfurt/M. 1999, pp. 157-174 (Zeitschrift für Bibliothekswesen und Bibliographie Sonderheft 75).

Griebel, R./Tscharntke, U. (1998): Etatsituation der wissenschaftlichen Bibliotheken 1997, Zeitschrift für Bibliothekswesen und Bibliographie 45, pp. 1-50.

Günther, J. (1999): Portfolio-Management, in: Controlling-Konzepte. Werkzeuge und Strategien für die Zukunft, hrsg. von E. Mayer u.a., 4. vollst. überarb. und erw. Aufl., Wiesbaden, pp. 192-210.

Haiber, T./Dunker, K. (1995): Kostenmanagement in öffentlichen Verwaltungen, in: Handbuch Kosten- und Erfolgs-Controlling, hrsg. von T. Reichmann, München, 472-497.

Hammer, M./Champy, J. (1996): Business Reengineering. Die Radikalkur für das Unternehmen, 6.Aufl., Frankfurt/M.

Hermann, U. (1996): Wertorientiertes Ressourcenmanagement. Neuausrichtung der Kostenrechnung aus ressourcenbasierter Sicht, Wiesbaden.

Hilke, W. (1989): Grundprobleme und Entwicklungstendenzen des Dienstleistungs-Marketing, in: Dienstleistungs-Marketing, hrsg. von W. Hilke, Wiesbaden, pp. 5-44 (Schriften zur Unternehmensführung 35).

Horváth, P./Mayer, R. (1993): Prozeßkostenrechnung - Konzeption und Entwicklung, Kostenrechnungspraxis 37, Sonderheft 2, pp. 15-28.

Horváth, P./Mayer, R. (1989): Prozeßkostenrechnung. Der neue Weg zu mehr Kostentransparenz und wirkungsvolleren Unternehmensstrategien, Controlling 1, pp. 214-219.

Hummel, S./Männel, W. (1990): Kostenrechnung 1: Grundlagen, Aufbau und Anwendung, 4. völlig neu bearb. und erw. Aufl. (Nachdruck), Wiesbaden.

Johnson, H.T./Kaplan, R.S. (1987): Relevance Lost. The Rise and Fall of Management Accounting, Boston, Massachusetts.

Kaeseler, J. (1996): Marktanalyse Geschäftsprozeßoptimierung. Softwarewerkzeuge zur Unterstützung der Geschäftsprozeßplanung und -optimierung, Dortmund.

Kajüter, P. (1997): Prozeßmanagement und Prozeßkostenrechnung, in: Kostenmanagement. Wettbewerbsvorteile durch systematische Kostensteuerung, hrsg. von Franz, K.-P./Kajüter, P., Stuttgart, pp. 209-231.

Kaufmann, L. (1997): Controllingorientierte Segmentierung von Prozessen, Kostenrechnungspraxis 41, pp. 211-217.

Kieninger, M. (1994): Wie man mit Prozeßzeitenmanagement die Durchlaufzeit senkt, in: Kunden und Prozesse im Fokus - Controlling und Reengineering, hrsg. von P. Horváth, Stuttgart, pp. 233-248.

Kilger, W. (1992): Einführung in die Kostenrechnung, 3. durchges. Aufl. (Nachdruck), Wiesbaden.

Koch, R. (1998): Das 80-20-Prinzip. Mehr Erfolg mit weniger Aufwand, Frankfurt/M.

Kommunale Gemeinschaftsstelle (KGSt) (1999): Abschreibungssätze in der Kommunalverwaltung, KGSt-Bericht 1/1999, Köln.

Kommunale Gemeinschaftsstelle (KGSt) (1998): Kosten eines Arbeitsplatzes (Stand 1997), KGSt-Bericht 7/1998, Köln.

Kommunale Gemeinschaftsstelle (KGSt) (1997): Von der Kulturverwaltung zum Kulturmanagement im Neuen Steuerungsmodell. Aufgaben und Produkte für den Bereich Kultur, KGSt-Bericht 3/1997, Köln.

Kommunale Gemeinschaftsstelle (KGSt) (1995): Arbeitszeit einer Normalarbeitskraft, KGSt-Bericht 5/1995, Köln.

Kranstedt, D./Wiemers, J. (1997): Internationales Netzwerk Öffentlicher Bibliotheken 4: Organisations-, Leistungs- und Kostenrechnung der Stadtbibliothek Paderborn, Gütersloh.

Künzel, E./Nickel, S./Zechlin, L. (1998): Verbindliche Maßstäbe fixieren. Zielvereinbarungen zwischen Staat und Hochschulen - das 'Neue Steuerungsmodell' im Blick, in: Wissenschaftsmanagement 4, pp. 24-27.

Küpper, H.-U. (1997): Hochschulrechnung zwischen Kameralistik und Kostenrechnung, in: Das Rechnungswesen im Spannungsfeld zwischen strategischem und operativem Management. Festschrift für Marcell Schweitzer zum 65. Geburtstag, hrsg. von H.-U. Küpper und E. Troßmann, Berlin, pp. 565-588.

Kuhnert, I./Leszczensky, M. (1998): Kostenrechnung an Hochschulen - Erfassung und Bewertung hochschulinterner Kostenstrukturen. Modellversuch an der Universität Bonn und der Universität-Gesamthochschule Wuppertal, hrsg. von der HIS GmbH, Hannover.

Kuhnert, I./Leszczensky, M. (1997): Kameralistisch basierte Hochschulkostenrechnung, HIS-Kurzinformation A7/97, Hannover.

Mayer, R. (1998): Prozeßkostenrechnung - State of the Art, in: Prozeßkostenmanagement. Methodik und Anwendungsfelder, hrsg. von der Horváth & Partner GmbH, 2. völlig neubearb. Aufl., München, pp. 3-27.

Mayer, R. (1996): Prozeßkostenrechnung und Prozeß(kosten)-optimierung als integrierter Ansatz - Methodik und Anwendungsempfehlungen, in: Kostenorientiertes Geschäftsprozeßmanagement. Methoden, Werkzeuge, Erfahrungen, hrsg. von C. Berkau und P. Hirschmann, München, pp. 43-67.

Mayer, R. (1991): Prozeßkostenrechnung und Prozeßkostenmanagement: Konzept, Vorgehensweise und Einsatzmöglichkeiten, in: Prozeßkostenmanagement. Methodik, Implementierung, Erfahrungen, hrsg. von der Horváth & Partner GmbH, München, pp. 73-99.

Meffert, H./Bruhn, M. (1997): Dienstleistungsmarketing. Grundlagen - Konzepte - Methoden, 2. überarb. und erw. Aufl., Wiesbaden.

Miller, G.J./Vollmann, T.E. (1985): The Hidden Factory, Harvard Business Review 63, pp. 142-150.

Müller, A. (1998): Gemeinkosten-Management. Vorteile der Prozeßkostenrechnung, 2. vollst. überarb. und erw. Aufl., Wiesbaden.

Naumann, U. (1998): Produktkataloge für Wissenschaftliche Bibliotheken, Zeitschrift für Bibliothekswesen und Bibliographie 45, pp. 295-311.

Niemand, St./Rassat, T. (1997): Marktorientiertes Dienstleistungsmanagement - ein qualitäts- und kostenorientierter Ansatz, in: Kostenrechnungspraxis 41, pp. 41-49.

Niemand, St. (1996): Target Costing für industrielle Dienstleistungen, München.

Olshagen, Ch. (1991): Prozeßkostenrechnung. Aufbau und Einsatz, Wiesbaden.

Paff, A. (1998): Eine produktionstheoretisch fundierte Kostenrechnung für Hochschulen - am Beispiel der Fernuniversität Hagen, Frankfurt/M.

Pirsich, V. (1997): Ham'mer längst! Kostenrechnung in Öffentlichen Bibliotheken - Möglichkeiten und Varianten, in: Buch und Bibliothek 49, pp. 772-792.

Poll, R./te Boekhorst, P. (1998): Leistungsmessung in wissenschaftlichen Bibliotheken. Internationale Richtlinien, München (IFLA Section of University Libraries & other General Research Libraries).

Pröhl, M./Windau, B. (Hrsg.) (1997): Betriebsvergleich an Öffentlichen Bibliotheken. Band 1: Empfehlungen und Arbeitsmaterialien für ein output-orientiertes Berichtswesen, Gütersloh.

Remer, D. (1997): Einführen der Prozeßkostenrechnung. Grundlagen, Methodik, Einführung und Anwendung der verursachungsgerechten Gemeinkostenzurechnung, Stuttgart.

Rendenbach, H.-G. (1997): Prozeßkostenmanagement in Versicherungen, in: Kostenmanagement. Wettbewerbsvorteile durch systematische Kostensteuerung, hrsg. von Franz, K.-P./Kajüter, P., Stuttgart, pp. 233-249.

Scheer, A.-W. (1998): ARIS - Vom Geschäftsprozeß zum Anwendungssystem, 3. völlig neubearb. und erw. Aufl., Berlin/Heidelberg.

Scheer, A.-W. (1997): Wirtschaftsinformatik. Referenzmodelle für industrielle Geschäftsprozesse, 7. durchges. Aufl., Berlin/Heidelberg.

Schoenfeld, H.M. (1997): Ressourcen Accounting - Ein Ansatz zur Erweiterung der Kostenrechnung, in: Kostenrechnung: Stand und Entwicklungsperspektiven. Wolfgang Männel zum 60. Geburtstag, hrsg. von W. Becker und J. Weber, Wiesbaden, pp. 429-445.

Serfling, K./Jeiter, V. (1995): Gemeinkostencontrolling in Dienstleistungsbetrieben auf Basis der Prozeßkostenrechnung, in: Kostenrechnungspraxis 39, pp. 321-329.

Stäglich, D. (1994): Finanzautonomie (Globalhaushalt) an nordrhein-westfälischen Hochschulen. Chance oder Risiko für Bibliotheken?, in: Arbeitsfeld Bibliothek. 6. Deutscher Bibliothekskongreß, 84. Deutscher Bibliothekartag in Dortmund 1994, hrsg. von H. Lohse, Frankfurt/M., pp. 236-248 (Zeitschrift für Bibliothekswesen und Bibliographie Sonderheft 59).

Staud, J. (1999): Geschäftsprozeßanalyse mit ereignisgesteuerten Prozeßketten. Grundlagen des Business Reengineering für SAP R/3 und andere betriebswirtschaftliche Standardsoftware, Berlin/Heidelberg.

Stößel, F.V. (1998): Outsourcing in der öffentlichen Verwaltung. Ein Instrument zur effizienteren Versorgung mit öffentlichen Gütern?, Frankfurt/M.

Umstätter, W./Rehm, M./Dorogi, S. (1982): Die Halbwertzeit in der naturwissenschaftlichen Literatur, Nachrichten für Dokumentation 33, pp. 50-52.

Volkert, W. (1996): Der Modellversuch 'Hochschule als Landesbetrieb' an der Fachhochschule Osnabrück, in: Globalhaushalte: Modelle und Erfahrungen, Dokumentation der Arbeitstagung der Technischen Universitäten Clausthal und Hamburg-Harburg vom 22. bis 24. Mai in Clausthal-Zellerfeld, Clausthal-Zellerfeld.

Vorschriftensammlung Bundesfinanzverwaltung VSF (1997): Stoffgebiet Haushaltsrecht, Abschnitt Kosten- und Leistungsrechnung. Bonn (KLR-Handbuch)

Wätjen, H.-J. (1994): Hochschulbibliotheken und Globalhaushalt am Beispiel Niedersachsens - Chancen und Risiken, Zeitschrift für Bibliothekswesen und Bibliographie 41, pp. 433- 446.

Weber, J. (1997): Einführung in das Rechnungswesen II: Kostenrechnung, 5. aktualis. und neugest. Aufl., Stuttgart.

Wewer, G. (1998): Globalisierung, Flexibilisierung, Budgetierung, in: Handbuch zur Verwaltungsreform, hrsg. von B. Blanke u.a., Opladen, pp. 289-295.

Zimmermann, G. (1992): Prozeßorientierte Kostenrechnung in der öffentlichen Verwaltung. Ein Ansatz zur Entgeltkalkulation und für ein wirkungsvolles Controlling?, Controlling 4, pp. 196-202.

Zwehl, W. v. (1997): Die Prozeßkostenrechnung als Informationsinstrument in der Kommunalverwaltung, Kommunale Steuer-Zeitschrift 46, pp. 201-210.